Guidance for
SUPPORTING
GENDER
DIVERSITY
in Early Childhood Education

Jenny Fererro, MS,
with
Rebecca Bishop

BULK PURCHASE

Gryphon House books are available for special premiums and sales promotions as well as for fund-raising use. Special editions or book excerpts also can be created to specifications. For details, call 800.638.0928.

DISCLAIMER

Gryphon House, Inc., cannot be held responsible for damage, mishap, or injury incurred during the use of or because of activities in this book. Appropriate and reasonable caution and adult supervision of children involved in activities and corresponding to the age and capability of each child involved are recommended at all times. Do not leave children unattended at any time. Observe safety and caution at all times.

DEDICATION

For all gender-creative children and the early childhood educators working to make their classrooms and programs inclusive and welcoming for **all** children.

TABLE *of* CONTENTS

FOREWORD

It would be unfair to share my story without acknowledging the incredible privilege I hold as a middle-class, light-skinned, cis-presenting woman living in a reliably blue state. So while I identify as biracial (Black/White), genderqueer (she/they), and neurodiverse (autistic), none of these identities are apparent to strangers. I find safety in ambiguity. The same is true for my eleven-year-old transgender son, Sunny. No one would mistake him for anything but a happy, healthy tween boy for whom the whole world is his oyster. The difference is that those strangers' first impressions of Sunny are 100 percent true.

I count Sunny and myself as lucky. We haven't suffered for our identities or been pushed to the margins because we choose to live out loud. We owe much (if not all) of our health, happiness, and safety to our privilege. But the impact of Sunny's privilege also serves as an example of what is possible when trans people's identities are affirmed by those closest to them: family, friends, teachers, religious leaders, and community.

Thus far, Sunny's story is uncommon, his childhood idyllic. When he first started showing clear preferences—for certain types of clothing, toys, and activities—at two years old, we figured he was trying to be more like his older brothers, not expressing his gender identity. Then, there were times when Sunny drew himself as a boy with short hair or refused to wear a dress for holiday pictures with Santa. All fine by us. He was barely out of diapers, so we thought, "What could Sunny know about gender?" His father and I were far more curious about than alarmed by Sunny's declarations, but we were also naive to how real and meaningful they were for him and his well-being.

Sunny was in kindergarten when he asked to cut his hair short and was in second grade when he asked for a suit and bowtie to wear to our church's holiday show. The signs that he didn't fit neatly into a binary gender box were all there. Eventually, with the guidance of two trans women in our community, my husband and I started attending a local PFLAG meeting for transgender adolescents and their families.

Around that time, I recalled a conversation I had had with my midwife during my pregnancy with Sunny. Louise didn't order routine ultrasounds, but we were anxious to know the sex of our fourth child, so we decided to get one on our own. Louise offered, "You can find out *what* you'll get but never *who* you'll get." She was right, thank goodness. Watching my five babies become full-grown people with opinions, passions, and dreams for the future surprises and nourishes me daily.

Louise's message wasn't just wise; it was prophetic. When Sunny came home from school one day not acting like himself, I knew something was very wrong. "They separated the boys and girls into different teams in gym today. I don't want to be with the girls," he said with eyes downcast. It was happening. Over the next several hours, Sunny shared what we had long anticipated. He wanted to change his name. He wanted to use he/him pronouns. He was a boy.

That was a Friday. We emailed his second-grade teacher, and she immediately began preparations to welcome *him* back to school on Monday. She would change the name tags on his desk and cubby and set up meetings for us to meet with the school's guidance counselors, principal, and vice principal. Sunny would use the bathroom of his choice, and his bus driver would be briefed on the update before Sunny was picked up on Monday morning. Everything was going to be okay. Like I said, lucky.

Our church, his guitar teacher, and his jiujitsu sensei responded with the same warmth and assurance that Sunny would be safe in their care. Not one member of our immediate or extended family batted an eyelash. Sunny was Sunny, and he was a boy—no big deal.

But being this lucky doesn't always feel good. I'm reminded of our exceptional experience constantly. Lawmakers seem to introduce another piece of anti-trans, anti-child legislation every day. Trans adolescents continue to hurt themselves because their communities refuse to accept them and their schools refuse to protect them.

I look at Sunny—a beautiful, happy, well-liked, curious child—and I can't imagine anyone would think there was anything *wrong* with him or kids like him. While writing this, I asked Sunny what being an eleven-year-old trans boy

is like, and he said, "I don't know, normal." What do his friends think? "Mom, it's no big deal. We don't talk about it. Danny asked me if I could turn into a robot, like a Transformer. It's a joke. Don't worry." This is eleven.

I don't believe Sunny's purpose is to prove trans people's humanity to those who doubt it, but I know that everyone in Sunny's life is better for knowing him. I know that when his friends hear a hateful lie about trans people, Sunny will come to mind as evidence that nothing so ugly could be true.

My hope for this book is that it will allow you, the reader, someone who loves, cares for, and teaches children, to know how critically important it is to affirm them in all the beautiful ways they express what makes them unique. Sunny's experience is uncommon and exceptional but a story every child deserves. It's our privilege as grown-ups to make sure the children in our care have every chance to be happy and healthy, to make the whole world their oyster. We'll all be better for it.

—Rebekah Borucki,
Author, publisher, mother to five

ACKNOWLEDGMENTS

We want to offer our sincere thanks and appreciation to the many parents and families who were generous with their time and trust in sharing their stories and perspectives.

Thank you to the early childhood educators and administrators who provided us with guidance, ideas, and anecdotes.

We appreciate the doctors, therapists, and gender advocates who provided us with important context for understanding the needs of gender-diverse children.

We are especially grateful to the gender-expansive children and young adults who shared their thoughts with us.

Jenny: I want to thank my colleagues at Palomar College for their support for the sabbatical in spring 2020 that led to this book. Many thanks to Camille Catlett and Sarah Garrity for their belief in the value of this work, their encouragement, and for connecting me with Gryphon House. Great love and appreciation to my family, especially my husband and daughter, for their continuing support. And most of all, thanks to my friend Becca for teaching me, believing in me, and partnering with me.

Rebecca: I am so grateful to Kathie Moehlig and Darlene Tando for their incredible support and to TransFamily Support Services for their dedication to the community. I want to thank my husband, Shane, and our children for their love and patience. A special thank you to my son who encouraged my participation in this book "to help other kids" and who reminded me when I worried about his privacy that I wasn't actually a movie star or something. Thank you for teaching me and keeping me humble. So much gratitude to the friends and family who have supported our experiences and grown with us. And thank you to Jenny who made this possible. I'm so honored to be part of anything you do.

GUIDANCE FOR SUPPORTING **GENDER DIVERSITY** IN EARLY CHILDHOOD EDUCATION

· x ·

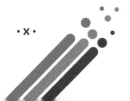

INTRODUCTION: A JOURNEY WITH GENDER

WHO ARE WE?

My name is Jenny Fererro, and I am a professor of child development and early childhood education and a former early childhood teacher. Most of my students are studying to become early childhood educators. I have been a professor for nearly twenty years, and I love helping my students become great teachers and develop a profound respect for children. My interest in gender diversity in early childhood was spurred by my friendships and personal relationships with parents of gender-diverse young children. I am a mother, a wife, a friend, a sister, a daughter, and more. My pronouns are she/her/hers.

My name is Rebecca Bishop*, and I am a mother of two. I worked previously in the early education field and currently work as a behavioral specialist for children with autism spectrum disorders. I am also an advocate for trans and nonbinary youth. My older daughter is cisgender. This means we identified her as female at birth, and she has continued to identify with that gender label. Our younger son is transgender. When our son socially transitioned in early childhood, my family and I found ourselves completely overwhelmed by the breadth of information and the lack of community education. Our family was given so many wonderful tools by therapists and advocates, but we consistently had to work hard to integrate what we knew into our son's play and school environments. My pronouns are she/her/hers.

*My decision to use a pseudonym was made with the support of my family to protect the privacy of my children.

WHO ARE YOU?

This book is written for early childhood providers: classroom teachers, aides and assistants, and administrators. If you are a person who works with children in the early years (birth to eight years), a parent, or a person interested in child development, then you may also find topics of interest here. While our focus is on classroom-based early childhood programs, families, nannies, and other home-based child-care providers can also benefit. At the end of the book are resources, including websites, books, and more.

Your picking up this book suggests that you are likely a person who is interested in learning more about children's gender development and may be open to exploring new ways of thinking about gender.

WHAT ARE YOU READING?

This book is designed to provide an introduction to working with and supporting young, gender-diverse children and their families. Rebecca's voice as a parent and advocate will be included throughout the book in Rebecca's Reflections.

This book has a focus on understanding and utilizing available resources. It is designed to provide you with the confidence to begin making changes in your classrooms and programs that will help create supportive and affirming environments for **all** your students. This is *not* an exhaustive resource, but rather a starting point for further growth and learning.

WHY IS THIS IMPORTANT?

We decided to write this book after recognizing the gap in knowledge related to gender issues that exists for many early childhood educators. While it

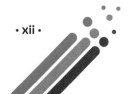

has become common practice to disrupt stereotyped gender roles by encouraging little girls to engage in outdoor play and little boys to use the dress-up area, many early childhood teachers may not truly understand gender identity development, and often feel unequipped to navigate conversations about gender, support families who have children who are gender creative, or to create classroom environments that are welcoming and supportive of children who are gender diverse. Within our circle of family, friends, and acquaintances, we know many families with young children who identify as transgender and socially transitioned in early childhood. These families are more common than most early childhood education (ECE) professionals think, and they deserve to be recognized and supported.

In 2014, President Obama signed Executive Order 13672, adding gender identity to the categories protected against discrimination in employment in the civilian and federal workforce. This executive order started an ongoing roller coaster of both gender-affirming and transphobic legislation throughout the United States. While the World Health Organization and the U.S. federal government recognize the validity of transgender and nonbinary identities, adults and children continue to be denied protection in many areas. Providing education about the developmental and scientific understanding of gender better equips teachers and families to share accurate information. Normalizing education around gender allows children to learn about gender and gender roles without conflating those with sex and sexuality and can help counter misinformation.

Based on census and population data, it is likely that one or more gender-expansive or LGBTQIA+ children is already enrolled in every child-care center or preschool in the country. It is simply not accurate to say, "I don't know any children like this." Transgender youth and gender diversity comprise an area of burgeoning research and interest—resources are multiplying by the year, and acceptance continues to grow. We want to provide a primer and help connect ECE professionals with resources they can use to help improve their teaching and programs. Studies show that children who are gender diverse who are supported at home and in school have far better outcomes than children who are not supported (more on this in Chapter 3). Supporting gender diversity in the classroom should be a regular part of best practice for ECE educators!

HOW TO USE THIS BOOK

We offer sections related to gender basics, tips for teachers, tips for administrators, affirming and best practices, support for families, resources, and more. It is recommended that those who are new to the topic begin with Chapter 1: Gender Basics, but the rest of the book is designed to be read in any order, depending on the needs of the reader. Please note that all ECE professionals will find useful information in Chapter 4: The Role of the ECE Teacher, and Chapter 5: The Role of the ECE Administrator. Throughout the book you will find Parent Perspectives, where parents of children who are gender diverse share their experiences and thoughts, and Youth Perspectives, where gender-diverse children and young adults share their opinions.

> Please note, throughout this book, *parents* refers to a child's primary adult caregivers, whether that is a sibling, another family member, a guardian, or other main adult.

Remember...

It is always best to learn from those you are learning about. In the past few years, multiple excellent resources compiled and written by gender-diverse authors have been published. There are many excellent resources available, both in print and on the internet, that can provide even more detail and expertise, depending on what you are hoping to learn. It is our hope that this book will help you begin your journey of expanding your understanding of gender, and that you will be inspired to continue to learn and grow.

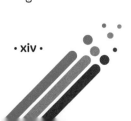

CHAPTER 1:
GENDER BASICS

SO, WHAT EXACTLY ARE WE TALKING ABOUT HERE?

One of the very first questions people ask when they learn of a new baby is "Is it a boy or a girl?" Most Americans think of gender as simple: people are either male or female, boy or girl, and those labels are tied to the body parts hidden by a bathing suit. Adults often teach children from a very early age, "Boys have penises and girls have vaginas." Ignoring the fact that this is an incorrect pairing—vaginas are internal organs, so it would be more correct to say, "Girls have vulvas"—this explanation of gender is vague and incomplete. A good illustration of the typical American perspective of gender is the common "gender reveal" parties held for pregnant women. Cut into the cake or pop the balloon, and blue icing or confetti means it's a boy; pink means it's a girl...

right? Not necessarily! It is impossible to tell a baby's gender identity from an ultrasound or diaper change.

Gender is complicated and much more nuanced than the binary boy/girl, blue/pink ideals that are so commonly advertised. And to best work with children and help them understand gender, adults need to understand these concepts themselves. It can be overwhelming to look at long lists of terminology and definitions, making it easy to throw up our hands and think that people are unnecessarily complicating something that is very simple. But as people who work with children, you care about understanding development, so let's learn!

GENDER 101: THE BASICS

At a very basic level, gender is what someone feels on the inside about who they are. It's not about body parts, clothing, or hairstyle. And gender has *nothing* to do with sexuality or sexual orientation. Gender is about identity and is tied to a person's sense of self. Gender exists on a spectrum; it is not just male or female. People can experience their gender at any place on that spectrum of gender identity. Assuming gender to be binary is not biological or even universal. Many cultures have *gender variances*, or more than two genders that are recognized and even celebrated. In nature, gender is fluid among many animal species, such as hyenas, colobus monkeys, clownfish, and seahorses.

Let's start with a little bit of terminology:

- **Gender:** social construction of personal identity

- **Sex:** physical characteristics and genetic makeup (what lives under the bathing suit and in the chromosomes). Sex is usually assigned at birth based on external genitalia.

- **Gender identity:** who a person is and how they see themselves (what lives in the brain)

- **Gender expression:** how a person is seen or expresses themselves through external appearance and behavior

> Gender is not the same as sex; identity is not the same as expression. And sexual orientation is separate from all of these.

Over the years, many attempts to simply illustrate the spectrums associated with the terminology around gender have been used and developed. One of the most widely accepted is the Gender Unicorn, developed by TSER (Trans Students Educational Resources https://transstudent.org).

Source: Trans Student Educational Resources. 2015.
http://www.transstudent.org/gender

Individuals can use the Gender Unicorn to help mark their own gender identity, expression, sex assigned at birth, physical attraction, and emotional attraction on the spectrum arrows. The infographic shows that identity is in the brain, attraction is in the heart, sex assigned at birth is in the genes and genitals, and expression is in the outward facing body, including hair, clothing, preferences, and behavior.

MEET US!

Hi, I'm Jenny. My **gender** is female, and my **sex** is also female. I am what's known as **cisgender**, meaning that my gender matches my chromosomal makeup and body. My **gender identity** is primarily female, but I also have parts of my identity that are more traditionally male: for example, I take pride in being the working parent in my family; I am the breadwinner. My **gender expression** is primarily female but is also fluid. I wear makeup and love bold lipstick and jewelry. I paint my nails all the time. I have had many very short hairstyles, often with shaved sides. I shop for clothing in both men's and women's sections of stores. I have personality traits and hobbies that are considered more traditionally female: for example, I love to bake, do needlework, shop, and gossip with friends. I also have some that are considered more traditionally male: I am outspoken and enjoy paddle outrigger canoeing. For the most part, my gender expression, identity, and gender all match with the sex I was assigned at birth.

I'm Rebecca and my **gender** is female and my **sex** is also female. I am **cisgender.** My **gender identity** is female, and I enjoy the parts of domestic life that are considered traditionally or stereotypically female. For example, I love being a stay-at-home mom, cooking dinner, taking the children to and from school, and maintaining our home. My **gender expression** is female, with many overlaps in what would be considered a more masculine style. I have short hair and lots of tattoos. I often wear gender-neutral clothes including jeans, men's sneakers and tees, and baseball hats. I rarely wear jewelry or accessories of any kind. I don't often dress up, but when I do, I favor a strong red lip and high heels. I have hobbies that are stereotypically female—like shopping—but most of my hobbies are nongendered, such as reading, photography, working out, and attending concerts. Overall, my gender expression, identity, and gender all match the sex I was designated at birth.

NAVIGATING TERMINOLOGY

It can be difficult to keep these different terms straight when you are first learning and exploring gender. It's also important to note that as understanding and practice evolve and broaden, terminology can become quickly outdated. Some terms are commonly used but are found by some groups to be offensive. While it can be challenging to keep abreast of current terminology, it is important to do so as an act of respect. An attempt is made here to provide definitions of some of the most common terms and words that you might hear or see, while indicating where controversy may lie at the time of this writing.

- **Agender:** A term referring to someone who does not identify as having a particular gender. People who are agender fall under the category of nonbinary.

- **Binary:** A term meaning "having two parts." When discussing gender, the term *binary* refers to the assumption and social construct that there are only two genders: male and female, which are strictly assigned at birth with no variants.

- **Biological Sex or Sex Assigned at Birth:** Biological sex is determined by internal/external reproductive sex organs, genes (sex chromosomes), and hormones. The term *biological sex* does not fully encompass the many

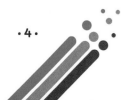

genetic, biological, and anatomical differences that can exist for people. Many people prefer the term *sex assigned at birth* (sometimes abbreviated as AFAB: "assigned female at birth" or AMAB: "assigned male at birth") or *legal designation* to illustrate that sex is usually assigned at birth based on external physical characteristics.

- **Cisgender:** A term referring to someone whose gender and identity correspond to their sex assigned at birth. *Cisnormativity* is the assumption that everyone is cisgender or that cisgender is the default. The prefix *cis* derives from a Latin root meaning "on this side of" and is an antonym for the prefix *trans,* derived from a Latin root meaning "across" or "beyond."

- **Gender:** A complex combination of identity, expression, sense of self, and social and legal status. Gender has three main components: identity, expression, and body.

- **Gender Attribution:** The process of individually assuming someone's gender, usually based on their name, voice, clothing, appearance, or behavior.

- **Gender Congruence:** The feeling of personal harmony in a person's gender

- **Gender Creative** (also **Gender Diverse**, also **Gender Expansive**): Terms referring to people, often children, who reject traditional gender roles, expression, or identity and express themselves in less binary ways

- **Gender Dysphoria:** A feeling of personal discomfort and disconnect in a person's gender

- **Gender Expression:** The external ways in which a person expresses their gender, often through clothing, behavior, and appearance

- **Gender Fluid:** People who identify as gender fluid move between genders. This is different than *agender*, which is more of a lack of a particular gender identity. People who are gender fluid fall under the category of nonbinary.

- **Gender Identity:** A personal sense of one's own gender. Tied to an individual's sense of self and how a person perceives themself and informed by the world around them. Gender identity can be fixed or can evolve over time for an individual.

- **Gender Identity Development:** A term referring to the developmental patterns and stages in human development related to gender identity and understanding; affected by biological, social, and environmental factors.

- **Gender Nonconforming:** Behavior or gender expression that does not fit easily into expected male/female behaviors and appearance. This term supports the idea of a gender binary, which means it implies that which does not conform to strict male/female lines is suspect. This term has been more recently replaced by **Gender Diverse, Gender Creative,** or **Gender Expansive**.

- **Gender Roles:** Societally defined expectations for appearance, behavior, actions, and values related to binary genders. Gender roles and their strictness can vary depending on culture, region, socioeconomic status, religion, ethnicity, and other factors.

- **Intersex:** People who are intersex are born with internal and/or external characteristics that differ from the binary expectation of male (XY chromosomes) and female (XX chromosomes). Intersexuality is common. Some estimates indicate that up to 2 percent of people born in the United States have variations in sex development (Blackless et al., 2000; https://isna.org/faq/frequency/). Many people who are intersex never know or do not learn that they are intersex until adulthood. Intersexuality does not have anything to do with gender, but it is common for people who are intersex to be misgendered.

- **LGBTQIA+** This acronym is used as an umbrella term to refer to people who identify as part of the community, encompassing lesbian, gay, bisexual, transgender, queer/questioning, intersex, asexual, with the + denoting the extensive identifying labels embraced by individuals within the community.

- **Misgender:** To misgender someone is to assume their gender incorrectly, often based on name, appearance, or voice.

- **Nonbinary:** A term referring to the spectrum of gender identities that are not exclusively male or female. To be nonbinary is to exist outside of the male/female binary structure.

- **Sexual Orientation:** A person's sexual identity and attraction. Orientations include *heterosexual* (sexually attracted to the opposite gender in a binary system), *homosexual* (attracted to the same gender in a binary system, also often referred to as *gay* or *lesbian*), *bisexual* (attracted to more than one gender), *polysexual* (attracted to multiple genders), *pansexual* (attracted to all genders without preference in a nonbinary system), *asexual* (lack of sexual attraction), and more. Sexual orientation is **not** dictated by or related to a person's own gender identity or expression.

- **Transgender:** A person whose gender identity does not correspond to the sex they were assigned at birth. Often abbreviated as *trans*. Although statistics are unreliable, as of 2016, around 0.6 percent of the US adult population is transgender (UCLA Williams Institute). Among US teens, 1.8 percent identify as transgender (CDC, 2019).

- **Transition:** The process for transgender people of choosing to live as the gender with which they identify rather than that assigned at birth. Transition can be *social* (name, pronouns, appearance) and/or *medical*

(hormone therapy and/or gender affirming surgeries). It's important to note that young children do not medically transition.

Perhaps the widespread cultural phenomenon of "gender reveals" should really be called "sex reveals," as the pregnant woman and her friends and family can only know the ultrasound's interpretation of external genitalia, not what the child's heart and brain will tell them about who they are.

GENDER EXPECTATIONS

In most of the world, including in the United States, children are surrounded by gender norms and expectations before they are even born. Studies have shown that expectant parents assign personality traits based on expected gender of their baby. For example, if the ultrasound tells them they are having a boy, kicks are described as *tough, strong*, and *active.* If the ultrasound showed a girl, those same kicks are described as signs that the baby will be a dancer. They speak differently in content and tone depending on whether they perceive their baby to be male or female (Brill and Pepper, 2008).

In Western culture, we assign male/female gender to behavior, language, colors, clothing, toys, sports, hobbies, careers, hairstyles, and more. Visit any toy store or big box retailer. Look at the colors in the aisles—almost without exception, dolls and pretend-play items are in aisles drenched in pink with advertisements featuring little girls. Building toys, action figures, and sports equipment are in aisles that are primarily black and blue with advertisements featuring little boys. Obviously, any child can enjoy any toy. In fact, you can probably think of examples from your own childhood of activities or toys you liked that didn't fit the expectations for your gender. As Anna Bianchi writes in *Becoming an Ally to the Gender-Expansive Child*, "all toys are gender neutral; it's the marketing of them that isn't" (2018). There is a slow-moving cultural shift that is starting. In California, AB 1084 was signed into law in 2021. This law will require large retailers to have designated sections for gender-neutral toys starting in 2024 (leginfo.legislature.ca.gov).

Children assimilate values and beliefs through the way adults consciously and unconsciously reinforce gender stereotypes and gender expectations. A parent who showers a daughter with compliments when she wears a frilly dress or a son when he shows skill on the playing field, but who remains silent or ambivalent about that same daughter wearing pants or the son enjoying art, is sending powerful messages about what behaviors and appearance are appropriate and admired. Most parents are unaware of the different ways they speak to and interact with children based on perceived gender, but it still happens. Due to this social conditioning, by age three most children show a preference for activities and toys associated with their gender (Brill and Pepper, 2008). Child-rearing practices, cultural beliefs and values, and societal expectations have often conspired to make children who are gender expansive or transgender hide their true selves. "When a child emerges as gender variant, the problem lies not with the child nor with its parenting, but with a society that places rigid limits on gender expression (Brill and Pepper, 2008).

Social-media videos of dads dressing as princesses with their daughters are meant to garner admiration for parents who flout gender conventions to please their child. And it is always wonderful when parents support their children! But it would be nice if it were the norm that activities, costumes, and clothes weren't gendered in the first place, so that videos like that weren't noteworthy enough to become viral.

Young children do not have negative views of other people's gender expressions or play unless it is communicated to them that it is "inappropriate." As early childhood professionals, we have the opportunity to ensure that our classrooms are safe spaces where children learn that all play is for all children. Learning about gender and gender variance will not make anyone trans or nonbinary, but it will allow for an environment where children can meet their potential without being stymied by gender norms. Later in this book, we explore tips for teachers and examples of great children's books that can help offset this pervasive binary gendering.

TALKING TO CHILDREN ABOUT GENDER

Some adults shy away from conversations about gender with children. They prefer to stick to binary boy/girl descriptors. But it is important to recognize that children have an understanding of gender that begins developing at the very earliest ages. In infancy, children begin internalizing the messages (both spoken and unspoken) that the adults around them communicate about gender. It is common for children to have questions about gender and to notice when what is shared with them doesn't match their own feelings or experiences. Children are learning about gender from the moment they are born, through the direct and indirect messages they are being sent by their parents, family, teachers, friends, and community.

> We have the opportunity to ensure that our classrooms are safe spaces where children learn that all play is for all children.

It's important to talk about gender early. The first three years are uniquely important in terms of brain development. Early experiences and feelings shape brain development. We want children to feel seen and understood, to know

they are respected, and to have the language and words to use to express their own feelings and experiences from the earliest ages. When gender is treated as a topic that is only appropriate for adults to discuss, children get the message that their experiences and feelings are not valid or are unimportant. Make sure that children have the opportunity to ask questions and share their feelings and ideas about gender. Adults often shy away from what they perceive to be "tough" conversations, but it is important to understand that children are observant and ready to learn about the world they are experiencing at a very early age.

As with any potentially complicated topic, remember to give children only the information they are asking for at the moment and to follow up with more information when they ask for more. Children are curious but are often very satisfied with simple answers and responses.

REBECCA'S REFLECTION

Because our son transitioned at a young age, it was important that our conversations surrounding his experience involve simple explanations and straightforward language. We imagined the various questions that would come up and how we'd navigate them, but we found, more often than not, that children were satisfied with our brief answers. It was also important for us to let our son know that many people don't "understand" gender diversity, and ignorant responses indicate lack of education or experience rather than being "their opinion" and possibly "right or wrong." The following is an example of part of a conversation we had with him:

As soon as we are born, the doctor makes a guess about our gender. They make a guess by some of the things they can see on the outside. A lot of times the doctors are right, but not always! Because gender identity is inside your body! Feeling like a girl or a boy or both or neither is something that only you can know. When a baby is born the doctor might say, "This is a boy!" If the child gets bigger and still feels and identifies as a boy, the child is cisgender. Sometimes though, a baby is born and the doctor might say, "This is a boy!" but the child might know inside, "I am a girl!" or "I am neither of those things!" They will need to tell their parents what they know about themselves so they can get a lot of support. This is their transgender (or nonbinary) experience. A person's gender is only one part of who they are—like their last name or their hair color—it doesn't have anything to do with what they like to play or what they are good at. It is important to treat everyone with kindness, no matter their gender identity. Friendship and fun and feeling included are things every kid deserves!"

Children deserve to have their observations about themselves and others acknowledged and responded to. Children may notice things about their peers that differ from their own understanding of gender: "Why is Josh wearing a skirt? Skirts are for girls." Resist the urge to shush or redirect children away from pointing out differences. Instead, use those opportunities to share an inclusive perspective: "Josh likes wearing a skirt. Skirts can feel very swishy and fun to wear. I like wearing skirts sometimes, and I also like wearing pants. What do you like to wear?" Think about framing conversations and observations related to gender expression as "some" or "many" rather than "all" or "always/never." Many girls have long hair, but not all. Some girls have pierced ears, and so do some boys. Using language that is inclusive can help steer children's comments away from gender absolutes. It's important for young children to know there is no one way to be any gender, and that people's experiences of gender can change over time. "Each individual is the expert on who they are, what they like, and how they want to show up in the world" (Pessin-Whedbee, 2019). Avoiding the use of terms such as "the other" or "the opposite" when talking about gender to children also helps emphasize the spectrum of gender rather than enforcing the binary.

Many adults are uncomfortable acknowledging gender diversity in young children. This is partially due to the fact that so many people equate and relate gender with sexual orientation. Nobody likes to think about young children and sex, so it is tempting to discount childhood gender diversity as being fictional or the creation of adults. It is common for adults to conflate gender and sexuality, leading adults to feel that children are "too young" to know their own gender identity or discuss gender. But gender is separate from sexual orientation. Many adults have grown up with their gender and their sexual orientation intertwined, so it can be hard to intuitively understand that they are not actually related. Talking about gender is **not** talking about sex. Gender is a topic that is appropriate for every age and can be handled in developmentally appropriate ways at home, in the community, and in the classroom.

PARENT PERSPECTIVES: WHAT PARENTS WANT YOU TO KNOW ABOUT GENDER

Parents of children who are gender diverse were kind enough to share their stories and experiences. When asked "What would you want adults working with young children to know about gender?" there were some striking similarities in their responses. Here is a selection:

> "Gender is a brain thing, not an anatomy thing."
>
> **—J, mother of a 13-year-old transgender son**

There are many wonderful children's books that can help adults start the conversation about gender with young children. Many of these books are appropriate for use in the classroom setting and are included in appendix B. Gender is a concept that children often have an easier time understanding than adults do. We can let the children lead the conversation and make sure that we are using appropriate vocabulary and respectful interactions. More specific tips are included in chapter 4.

> Talking about gender is **not** talking about sex. Gender is a topic that is appropriate for every age and can be handled in developmentally appropriate ways.

DISCUSSING ANATOMY

It is important to talk to young children about their anatomy using appropriate and accurate terminology. Although some adults feel uncomfortable using words like "penis" and "vulva" with children, it is important that children know the accurate names for their body parts. Children who know the accurate names for their body parts are better able to advocate for themselves and describe any issues that may arise, including medical needs or situations involving abuse. Just as we wouldn't be embarrassed to teach an infant that the features on their face include eyes, nose, and mouth, we shouldn't avoid teaching them appropriate names for their genitals.

Genitalia is only one aspect of a person's anatomy, and anatomy does not always match with gender identity. We can be careful about the way we discuss anatomy to help children feel included. Avoid making absolute statements that assume homogenization or the binary (for example, "All girls have vaginas.") Instead, you can talk about body parts in less finite terms. "Some bodies have vulvas, and some bodies have penises."

The book *Supporting Gender Diversity in Early Childhood Classrooms* is a good resource for further exploration of these conversations (Pastel et al., 2019).

"This [gender diversity] is a human variance just like eye color or hair color. Being trans is not a choice; people are born with it."

—H, mother of a 14-year-old transgender son and a 12-year-old cisgender daughter

"[Teachers] have to understand that gender is in your brain—it's not your genitalia or sexual orientation."

—K, mother of an 18-year-old transgender daughter

"That gender is a spectrum, and while many/most kids are cisgender, **all** children are on their own gender journey in one form or another. Learning about gendered and/or nonbinary expression is so valuable for **any** child. Also, I wish more adults, especially those working with children, understood the nuances and distinctions between expression, identity, and sexuality."

—C, mother of a 7-year-old transgender daughter and a 9-year-old cisgender son

"Believe kids and follow their lead no matter what you think about it."

—K, mother of a 20-year-old transgender son and an adult cisgender daughter

"We don't always know what gender a kid is by what they choose to wear or the clothes, name, pronouns that have been chosen for them. It is important to listen to each child. Let the children lead."

—L, mother of a 7-year-old transgender daughter

"I used to think that traditionally in early childhood, children were born a specific gender and they were too young to understand otherwise. The longer I worked in ECE, the more my perspective changed. At a very early age, children can demonstrate specific gender expression, and in seeing this I began to see how stifling the traditional mindset must be for those children to develop and be secure in who they are."

—C, ECE professional and mother to a nonbinary adult child

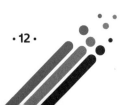

"Gender is an expression. Your expression is yours and other people (children, too) can teach you about theirs. Honor each child's expression and respect their choices in language."

—S, mother of a 7-year-old transgender son

"Kids don't make up their gender or say things for no reason. Believe children when they tell you who they are. Whether you 'agree' or not, you need to support children where they are."

—R, mother of a 5-year-old transgender son and a 7-year-old cisgender daughter

"Gender neutral doesn't mean taking away children's gender."

—M, mother of a 10-year-old gender-creative child, a 12-year-old cisgender son, and a 5-year-old cisgender daughter

"Through my child I have come to learn that gender is not black and white. My child knew at the age of three that their gender assigned at birth was wrong. Society has created a gender binary and oppressed anyone that doesn't fit into the tiny box given to them at birth. There is something incredibly beautiful about watching and supporting a child [in] knowing who they are and asking for the changes they need to be their most authentic self."

—S, mother of a 6-year-old transgender son and three cisgender children

YOUTH PERSPECTIVES:
WHAT GENDER-DIVERSE KIDS WANT YOU TO KNOW ABOUT GENDER

"The most important thing you can instill in children is doubt that the status quo is the best way. Standing up for children who are getting bullied, providing them support, and letting them know they didn't do anything wrong or actually worthy of ridicule means so much to them and would've meant so much to young me. And it's fine and great that most kids who feel comfortable exploring their gender options will ultimately come to the conclusion that they're cis; it's just important for the kids who ARE trans to not feel too scared to even think about possibly being trans, and then not feel too scared to explore their gender."

—G, college student (he/him)

"Gender does not exist. Gender is mostly about stereotypes."

—N, age 9 (he/him/his)

GENDER DEVELOPMENT

DEVELOPMENTAL UNDERSTANDING OF GENDER IDENTITY

Some adults find it hard to believe that a young child can have a strong sense that their gender is different than that which they've been assigned. It's common to hear "They're too young to know." Parents who support their young children in socially transitioning are often faced with pushback, accusations of abuse, and allegations that they are forcing their child to be a different gender. What's important for those who work with children to understand is that young children have a very strong sense of who they are, even before they have language to talk about it. Studies published by the American Academy of Pediatrics (AAP) have shown that children have a solid understanding of their own gender before the age of four. A child is never too young to know who they are inside. Think back for yourself—when did

> **Young children have a very strong sense of who they are, even before they have language to talk about it.**

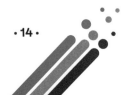

> "When I was born, the doctor said I was a girl because they didn't know me that well and I couldn't tell them yet... I am a boy on the inside of my tummy and my brain, and I just got born before my body finished growing the boy outside stuff."
>
> **—O, age 3, (he/him/his)**

> "I wish that they [adults] wouldn't just say 'it's a girl' or 'it's a boy.' I wish they'd wait because if they are wrong the kid could feel hurt, disappointed, or left out."
>
> **—W, age 7 (he/him/his)**

> "If a child says that they are transgender, it's important to be respectful and also patient with them. They could always realize later on that their gender identity is actually different, and it's perfectly fine for that to happen—some people won't realize their gender right away and they might keep changing their mind. This doesn't mean that their identity is invalid."
>
> **—R, age 19 (he/him/his)**

you know you were the gender you are? Most cisgender people can't even remember a time that they didn't know they were their gender. The same is true for many people who are transgender or gender diverse.

MILESTONES

Here are some developmental milestones related to gender identity and understanding of gender. You may be surprised to see how young children are when they start to show signs of gender recognition!

INFANTS (0-18 MONTHS)

- By three to four months, infants can distinguish between male and female faces (Pickron and Cheries, 2019).

- At six months, infants are able to discriminate between the faces and voices of men and women (Miller, Younger, and Morse, 1982).

- Between ten and eighteen months, infants start to form stereotypic associations between gender-typed objects and male/female faces, for example "matching" the hammer with the man's face and the dress with the woman's face (Martin and Ruble, 2010).

- By twelve months, infants begin to categorize individuals by gender (Quinn et al., 2002). They can match female voices to female faces and male voices to male faces and look longer at the faces that "match" the voice they are hearing (Spears Brown, 2014).

- By sixteen months, babies can label the gender of their parents (Spears Brown, 2014).

TODDLERS (18 TO 36 MONTHS)

- Starting in infancy and by thirty months, toddlers are able to categorize themselves and others by gender (Zosuls et al., 2009).

- By eighteen months, children begin to understand their own gender identity (Halim, Bryant, and Zucker, 2016).

- By two years old, most children know the gender group to which they and others belong.

- By two years old, children are able to communicate an awareness that their gender identity is different than their legal designation (the gender they were assigned at birth) (Steensma et al., 2011).

- By two years old, children begin to recognize gender stereotyping and show an expectation for children to present gender according to binary gender norms (Zosuls et al., 2009).

- By thirty months, most toddlers can communicate about their gender identity using language (Halim, Bryant, and Zucker, 2016).

- By age three, children are using gender pronouns to refer to themselves consistently (Nealy, 2019).

Toddlers express a desire to categorize their world and often resist gender variant expressions in adults or others. A common toddler task (and developmental skill) is sorting—and toddlers are often adamant about sorting people into tidy categories.

Erik Erikson, a twentieth-century developmental psychologist, was well known for his theories on lifespan psychosocial development. Erikson felt that rather than being fixed, a person's personality is shaped throughout their life through their experiences and social relationships. According to Erikson, toddlers are in the stage of autonomy vs. shame and doubt. During this stage of development, children are discovering the separation of self from others and developing their sense of self (Orenstein and Lewis, 2021). Their burgeoning autonomy is often seen in the child's language use. For example, children may start refusing certain types of dress or toys using language rather than just actions.

PRESCHOOLERS (THREE TO FIVE YEARS)

- By the age of three, most children are aware of anatomical differences and may start implementing gender segregation in play and socialization (Martin and Ruble, 2010).

- During preschool, children associate gender with particular behaviors and commonly use gender scripts (for example, "Boys don't play with dolls.").

- Most children are fairly stable in their gender identity by the age of four.

- Self-stereotyping related to gender traits starts early in life. By age six, girls are less likely than boys to think that members of their gender are highly intelligent (Joel and Vikhanski, 2019).

- Before the age of six or seven, children often believe that gender is determined by clothing and hairstyle (Nealy, 2019).

- Many trans people remember realizing before the age of five that their gender was different from their assigned sex at birth (Yong, 2019).

According to Diane Ehrensaft, a renowned expert on gender-diverse children, in her book *The Gender Creative Child* (2016), "[D]evelopmentally, at age six or before, all children are quite capable of knowing their gender. That does not mean this self-identity will remain stable throughout their entire lifetime, but it does mean, on average, children will exhibit a core consistency and cohesion of self… ." In the mid-twentieth century, psychologist Lawrence Kohlberg joined the ranks of theorists focusing on child development. For more than half a century, Kohlberg's theory of gender constancy was widely accepted. Kohlberg posited that children realize at a young age that their gender is fixed and does not change (Ruble et al., 2007). Although Kohlberg's ideas about how children perceive gender have been discounted in recent years, the idea that children's gender does not change over time remains active in many developmental circles. Reliance on outdated theories can result in a more rigid or fixed understanding of development. However, research and studies show that gender can and does evolve throughout a person's life.

"Unquestionably, there are multiple factors that affect gender identity, from the biological to the sociological, and while there are still many questions to be answered, what we know now is that the interaction of genes with prenatal exposure to hormones in the second half of pregnancy affects brain development in such a way that it significantly influences gender identification. Recognizing that the sexual differentiation of a fetus's brain happens later in pregnancy than genital differentiation and that both are complex biological processes, the fact that variations in gender identity exist should ultimately come as no surprise" (Ellis Nutt, 2016).

Gender socialization theory (Carter, 2014) proposes that gender is taught and enforced by external sources. Adults and caregivers directly shape a child's understanding of gender by reinforcing or punishing their behavior. Schools and social institutions set up gender-normed expectations for appearance, behavior, and interests and enforce these expectations in various ways throughout the environment. This concept stems from theories about gender understanding proposed by Kohlberg (1966) and Bussey and Bandura (1999) that focus primarily on external enforcers for gender identity. However, cognitive perspective theory posits that children play an active role in understanding their own and others' gender using *schemas*, or blueprints for understanding formed by patterns of repeated behavior and created through experience and exploration.

Many scientific studies have helped shape our current understanding of how gender develops. While it was previously thought that gender was entirely a social construct and was socialized into children, researchers and scientists now know that while socialization plays a powerful role in gender expression and identity, there are aspects of gender that are "hard-wired" into the brain. The influence of prenatal hormones seems to play a role, and neurological research is continually finding more evidence for physical markers of gender in the brain. Studies are showing that gender appears to be genetically coded, like handedness, eye color, and other traits, and that gender areas in the brain are mosaic, meaning that gender identity is affected by parts of the brain or even specific synaptic connections that emerge after the physical genitalia develop prenatally (Joel and Vikhanski, 2019).

According to the *Report of the 2015 U.S. Transgender Survey*, 32 percent of transgender people surveyed began to feel before the age of five that their gender was different than what was assigned on their birth certificate; another 28 percent began feeling that difference between the ages of six and ten (James et al., 2016). Children know who they are, often long before they can or want to communicate that knowledge.

TRANSGENDER AND GENDER-EXPANSIVE CHILDREN

Many children are gender expansive. Some are transgender. All transgender children are gender expansive, but not all children who are gender expansive are trans. Transgender issues have been in the spotlight more than ever in recent years. With that growing attention, understanding and awareness are also increasing. Many transgender people know at young ages that their birth gender does not match their gender identity.

REBECCA'S REFLECTION

My son (identified female at birth based on visible genitalia) began walking at seven months and was talking by eleven months. When he was a year-and-a-half old, he started self-identifying as a boy. We corrected him again and again. Each time he would cry or shake his head and say, "I's a boy! I is! I know!" We threw around terms like "tomboy" and "not super girly" in an effort to see where the disconnect was. He began hiding traditional girl clothes—taking them from his dresser or hamper and putting them in his sister's room. When playing with peers, he would become upset at being labeled a girl or assigned a girl role (princess, mommy, queen). Toilet training was difficult because he did not like having to sit to pee, and he insisted on lying on his stomach during diaper changes. He once shouted at an employee in Trader Joe's who complimented my beautiful daughters, "But I am a son!" He was insistent, consistent, and persistent in his gender identity, even as a toddler. By age three we were working closely with therapists and his pediatrician as his insistence led to severe dysphoria and he was hiding, listless, or attempting self-harm much of the time. His self-worth, development, and physical safety became increasingly dependent on our allowing this initial social transition by changing pronouns. A week or so after his third birthday, we asked, "If you don't feel like our daughter, who do you feel like?" He said, "A son, a nephew, a brother, a grandson, a boy, a boy." My husband asked him, "What do you want me to call you?" and our son said, "I just want you to say, 'I love you, my boy.'" And we do, so we did. We changed pronouns—just dropped the s from *she* and the r from *her*—and he blossomed. Within one week he had drawn his first self-portrait, toilet-trained, and with a fresh haircut exclaimed in the bathroom mirror, "I is me!!" Allowing him to lead us when we weren't sure where we were going was challenging. While children don't have functional autonomy until young adulthood, they have internal sense of self and emotional and behavioral autonomy by ages two to three. This means my son, like most children, had a strong understanding of who he was before he had the language. It became a big part of my goal as a parent and educator to advocate for all children to have the opportunity to be heard.

Whereas in the past, parents were encouraged to force their children into traditional gender expression aligning with their gender assigned at birth, the tide is slowly turning. The most up-to-date evidence, research, and science shows that children who are affirmed in their gender identity have the best outcomes (more on this in chapter 2). More and more families are feeling supported in helping their child socially transition at early ages, including in early childhood. As early childhood professionals, it is almost guaranteed that you have, or will have, children in your classrooms who are gender expansive or even transgender.

> I *thought* I gave birth to two penis-having boys, initially. And my transgender daughter is my younger child, so we didn't already have "girl stuff" around the house. My older son never dabbled in gender-variant play whatsoever when he was young, but he also didn't gravitate toward typically male toys

and other things either—it's worth noting that he is autistic, so his interests and expressions have always been a little extreme and obsessive and not necessarily especially traditional, in a gender sense or otherwise. My daughter basically came into the world reaching for princess items and wanting to be near anything pink, sparkly, and feminine from the earliest age she could express herself. At twenty-two months, she threw a tantrum in the aisles of Target when I tried to make her pick the Olaf costume (from *Frozen*, her favorite movie)—screaming and crying "Nooooo! Annnaaaaa! I only beee Aaaannnaaaa!!" So she got to be Anna—and she BEAMED with joy that Halloween night. From then on, her collection of dress-up dresses, nightgowns, fairy wings, and Barbies only grew—because I, frankly, never had a problem with it. I assumed she would grow out of it, but even if she didn't then we'd roll with it. (Spoiler alert: she didn't!)

Early on, people thought it was sort of cute, because they assumed it was a phase, I think. However, the longer her "girl-based" interests/dress/play continued (starting at age one and continuing and intensifying from there each year), folks definitely became more "concerned" and wondered what was going on. My husband reacted initially by being more firm about making our child wear boy clothes, play sports, watch more masculine cartoons, etc., thinking that she just needed more male-centric examples. It definitely didn't work. All it did was alienate her from her father for a long period of time (he ultimately came around and now embraces her identity completely). My daughter's preschool teachers didn't try to stop her from doing "girl things," they just shrugged their shoulders and let her do what she wanted (to my knowledge, there hadn't been a very gender-variant kiddo there before) and didn't make a big deal out of it."

—C, mother of a 7-year-old transgender daughter (E), and a 9-year-old cisgender son

Children who are gender expansive can present in multiple ways. Many young children enjoy activities and dress that are outside the gender norms for their assigned gender. When Jenny was a preschool teacher nearly twenty years ago, she had numerous children in her classes who showed distinct preferences for activities, playmates, and dress that flouted conventional gender norms, including four-year-old Robert, who made a beeline for the dress-up area the moment he entered the classroom. There, he would claim

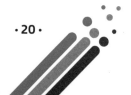

a pair of slip-on high heels, a flouncy tulle skirt, and sometimes a cape. Once dressed, he would go about the rest of his preschool day in his shoes and skirt. He was supported by his preschool teachers in his preferences, and the other children were also accepting. Jenny mentioned Robert's love for specific dress-up at his parent-teacher conference. Her observations were shared as one of many examples of how Robert enjoyed preschool. His mother, a glamorous woman who was a professional flamenco dancer, shared that Robert probably wanted to dress like she did. It's unknown what Robert's adult gender identity is. But we know that he was supported at home and at school in exploring his preferences that existed outside of gender stereotypes and norms.

Twenty years ago, the term *transgender* was not commonly used, and it certainly was not used in the context of talking about preschool-age children. Today, the terminology is more common, but adults often have a hard time accepting that children can express an understanding of their gender that would qualify them as transgender. However, some young children express very adamantly that they are not the gender that was assigned to them at birth. They may insist on being called a different name and/or express a preference for pronoun usage. Some children reject clothing or toys that are provided to them based on their assigned gender. Some exhibit self-harming behaviors or show mental distress around their body parts or clothing. But others simply lack a way to feel comfortable enjoying their preferred clothing and activities. Aidan Key, a well-respected gender educator and advocate who is the founder of Gender Spectrum, shared at the Gender Odyssey 2019 conference that sometimes children feel they have to be a different gender to do the things they like to do or look the way they want to look. Once they learn that there are many options and are freed from stereotypes, they are often comfortable with who they are. The vast majority of gender-diverse children are not transgender, and assuming that all children who are gender creative are trans, or will be trans, is problematic. What is important is to provide young children the space to be who they are.

> "Well, it's not a big deal. It's kind of private, not really school stuff or important there. It's when a boy has a vulva or a girl has a penis or someone only has one but feels like both. But that's it. That's all that's different."
>
> —W, 7-year-old transgender boy, when asked how to explain what *transgender* is to someone who doesn't know

Because so many adults, including health and educational professionals, erroneously insist that children are "too young" to know who they are, often one of the first and biggest obstacles that gender-expansive children face is getting the adults in their lives to see them for who they are. Many young children who are transgender will be hypergendered in their gender expression, insisting on the most stereotypically gendered clothes and toys as they attempt to assert their gender, but will settle into less rigid expressions once they feel secure that they are accepted and seen.

> "Our friends, nanny, and extended family were generally very supportive. However, we found that many did, and do, need more time to educate themselves. Even for those who are 'supportive,' they often lack a knowledge of gender expansiveness in young children. Some said it outwardly, and others we could read between the lines, but there was a sense that we were 'rushing' or that she was 'just so young.'
>
> Unfortunately, what is most persuasive to many seemed to be stories of our child's dysphoria and distress. As a parent, I wish we trusted gender-expansive children when they simply said, 'No, I'm not a _____. I'm _____.' There shouldn't need to be in distress for a child to be believed. No one thinks twice when a cisgender child affirms their gender assigned at birth, but we are still so far from trusting gender-expansive children in the same way."
>
> —D, father of a 4-year-old transgender daughter and a 2-year-old child

The TransYouth Project is a large-scale, longitudinal study of transgender youth being conducted by Kristina Olson and her team at the University of Washington. Research coming out of the TransYouth Project shows that transgender children's sense of self and identity is as strong as that of cisgender children. Transgender children's development mirrors that of cisgender children, and they show no developmental differences, particularly when raised in a supportive and affirming environment (Gülgöz et al., 2019).

One way that medical professionals help families determine whether their child might be exploring gender-diverse play and dress or might actually be transgender is considering whether the child is consistent, persistent, and insistent. Are they *consistently* behaving in gender-diverse ways? Are they *persistent* in their behavior? Are they *insistent* that their assigned gender is incorrect? These are all signs that the child may be transgender. Parents are also often asked to consider their child's preferred toys, preferred swimsuit/

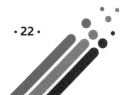

underwear (or a swimsuit aversion), and preferred method of urination. While a child who is consistent, persistent, and insistent in wanting "opposite gendered" toys, swimsuits or underwear, and method of urination is often a child who is transgender, it's important to note that play preferences alone are not typically indicative of future gender identity. There are infinite reasons a child may want to engage in "opposite gender" play or expression.

REBECCA'S REFLECTION

When our son was very small, his clothes were primarily made up from his sister's hand-me-downs. He hated tights and shiny shoes. He would tuck his dresses into his diaper or pinch the skirt between his legs. We found he had been "returning" clothes to his sister's room until all that was left were a few nongendered tees and leggings. We accepted hand-me-downs from friends so he had more clothes he preferred—sweatpants and superhero tees and anything with dinosaurs or cars. He was an insistent Boy Anna to his sister's Elsa and a king to her queen. When his older sister painted her nails, he refused, and he would shriek if he had marker or food coloring on his nail beds, "I is a boy! Get it off!" Once a marathon bath taker, he started requesting showers so he wouldn't have to look at his body. He wanted complete privacy getting dressed, even as he struggled with the developmental effort of donning long-sleeved tees and snug pant legs and putting on socks. He was reluctant to toilet train, especially due to an inability to go standing up, and would lie on his stomach for diaper changes. He still played with many of his sister's dolls but began asking more often for Matchbox cars and dinosaurs (although his play remained firmly family centered—with Matchbox babies and dinosaur weddings). What was so funny to me was that even as people questioned his identity and ability to "know," they validated his play as being indicative of something more serious. "Huh, he still plays with Barbies... I bet he will change his mind back." Or, better still, "Whoa! He is serious about that car collection. Guess he's all boy after all!" The reality is many transgender children will assert an interest in clothes, toys, and activities that align with their gender identity. It can be due to true interest, but it can also be a message: "Look how loud I am being a (boy/girl)!" What we found was that, about two years after our son transitioned, he started letting his sister put makeup on him to be silly and trying on my old clothes and heels for funny fashion shows. When I asked him, "Why are you okay wearing makeup now but not when you were little?" He said, "Because now everyone knows I'm really a boy so it's not a big deal. I'm just playing around."

Children who are transgender are born transgender. Adults and environment cannot make a child be truly transgender, although parenting and environmental pressures can cause children to choose gender-nonconforming dress and play. Biological theories that "explain" transgenderism and gender diversity include prenatal hormone exposure, DNA variations, brain development differences, and others. In *The Transgender Child*, one of the preeminent books about children who are trans and their development, the authors make the case for biological causes of transgenderism. "From this perspective, the brain is a gendered organ, and gender identity is not a conscious decision. People do not choose to feel like a boy or a girl, or like both, or neither. They simply are who they are" (Brill and Pepper, 2008).

REBECCA'S REFLECTION

When our son first struggled with his gender identity, we were lucky to have a small group of close friends who witnessed firsthand much of what we were experiencing. But life is not a vacuum, and the longer he struggled, the more we needed to share, to ask for help, and to create safe spaces for him. Sharing what was happening with people who hadn't seen him regularly was difficult. It was my first introduction into how charged people feel about this issue. My husband and I felt like we were discovering something tremendous while everyone else just thought we were failing, or at the very least, falling for something. They said it was just because he was close to his dad or because his sister was so feminine. They said to ignore him but definitely get him in sports. They said he was confused. They said, "When I was little, I wanted to be a cat!" or "I thought I was a princess when I was his age!" It was crushing to realize that my son could be struggling and we could be desperate for support and that people could simply not believe us.

By the time he was two-and-a-half and had failed to convince us and our community, he spent much of his time hiding under a blanket, even carrying it with us in the car, so people wouldn't look at him, so they couldn't "guess wrong" about him. One afternoon we were driving home and he asked me from the backseat, "Mama, would you like me to pretend? Would it be better if I pretended? If I pretended I was a girl would it be easier? But can I still be me inside and you will still know I'm a boy?" That was the point when my husband and I realized he was exhausted by all this, so sincere and broken down that we could not continue to fail him. Our pediatrician and the therapists we had been working with all agreed that allowing our son to use his preferred name and pronoun could be lifesaving, even if it wasn't life changing. Our son transitioning wasn't about being transgender at first—it was about allowing him to grow as his most authentic self.

When we told people that we had made a decision to honor our son and meet him where he was at, we were met with shock that we would allow our son to "choose" his gender at such a young age. This felt heartbreaking. As his parents, the transition and choice had been ours. Recognizing what our son knew about himself and advocating for his right to openly express his gender identity felt like a very long and private journey that, by its nature, we had to share with everyone. The more often I shared specifics of what this felt like for us, what this looked like for us, the more people began to understand how unique and fragile these situations are. We have politicized the idea of gender, even though science shows that what we currently know is limited and not so black and white (or so boy and girl). The reality is that gender is a deeply individual thing and denying children the ability to explore what it means for them can have an impact on their self-esteem and sense of worth.

Luckily, parents and teachers do **not** need to feel 100 percent confident in a child's gender identity or know the causes of it to affirm and support the child's choices and preferences. You can be supportive regardless of your own certainty or lack thereof. Affirming a child's identity can only help that child in the long run, while rejecting a child's assertions about who they are can cause long-term harm.

PRONOUN PRIMER

Pronouns are an important part of gender identity and a way for people to show respect for people and their gender. Traditionally, male pronouns are

he/him/his, and traditionally female pronouns are *she/her/hers*. But there are other options for pronouns that people may prefer when the traditional pronouns don't feel right. These are known as gender-neutral or gender-inclusive pronouns. Gender-inclusive pronouns can seem awkward or unfamiliar to those who are unused to them. But they offer an opportunity for people to find personal pronouns that fit who they are and feel good to them.

The pronouns *they/them/theirs* can apply to anyone. Although these pronouns are often thought of as being plural, they do not need to be. Some people choose to use the singular *they* exclusively, but some use a mix of pronouns, for example, *he/they*. It's common in English to use the singular *they* when we don't know someone's pronouns. If someone leaves their bag on a bench and you didn't see who left it, you might ask "I wonder when they'll come back for their bag?"

While *they/them/theirs* is the most common gender-neutral pronoun set, there are other gender-inclusive pronouns that, while potentially less familiar to the general public due to a lack of usage in mainstream media, are growing in popularity, especially among young adults and teenagers. Here are just a few examples of what are known as *neopronouns*:

HE/SHE	HIM/ HER	HIS/ HER	HIS/ HERS	HIMSELF/ HERSELF
they	them	their	theirs	themself
e	em	eir	eirs	emself
zie	zim	zir	zis	zieself
ve	ver	vis	vers	verself
tey	ter	tem	ters	terself
sie	sie	hir	hirs	hirself
fae	faer	faer	faers	faerself

WHY BOTHER?

Pronoun usage matters. Using people's correct personal pronouns makes them know that you see them and that they are respected. Some people feel that alternative pronouns are silly or wrong, but using preferred or chosen pronouns is a very basic way to prevent someone from feeling alienated or disrespected. "It is a privilege to not have to worry about which pronoun

someone is going to use for you based on how they perceive your gender. If you have this privilege, yet fail to respect someone else's gender identity, it is not only disrespectful and hurtful but also oppressive" (LGBTQ+ Resource Center, 2022). It is an aggressive act to purposely or continually use the wrong pronouns or use gendered language (*ma'am, sir*) when you have been informed or corrected. Use neutral language whenever and wherever possible until you know otherwise.

It is common to make mistakes, especially when someone you know changes their pronouns. Making a mistake and correcting yourself is always okay; purposely using the wrong pronouns is not, even if you believe the person should use certain pronouns. You can't always tell what pronouns someone uses just by looking at them. Using neutral pronouns such as *they/them/their* or using someone's name until you know someone's pronouns is best. The easiest way to know what pronouns someone prefers is to ask them, "What pronouns do you use?" It is also a good idea to share your own pronouns: "My name is Morgan; my pronouns are *she/her/hers*." This indicates that you welcome learning about other people's pronouns. Sharing your own pronouns is a very simple way to identify yourself as an ally, a safe person, and someone who cares about the people you are interacting with (Cory, Fererro, Sadat Ahadi, 2021). Normalizing the use of the singular *they* to refer to book characters or people you don't know also helps to show children and others that gender does not always need to be assumed.

It's important to note that not all languages use gendered pronouns. American Sign Language (ASL) is one example of a language without gendered pronouns. However, for those teachers and classrooms that use primarily English, Spanish, or other languages that do rely on gendered pronouns, it's valuable to pay attention to ways to respect individual choices related to pronouns. A great resource for those who are looking to learn more about personal pronoun usage is https://www.mypronouns.org/

WHAT ABOUT CHILDREN'S PRONOUNS?

Children also have preferred pronouns. Very young children may not know that they have options but can definitely feel that some pronouns are wrong for them. Just as with adults, you can tell the children how you like to be referred to and ask them what they prefer. Some young children will not show a preference in their personal pronouns. It is common for elementary and older children to be more specific about pronoun usage, but while younger children are most likely to show distinct preferences about gender labels ("I'm not a girl. I'm a boy!"), it is not unheard of for toddlers and preschoolers to also be adamant about which pronouns they prefer.

Opening the door to conversation about pronouns by sharing your own can help children feel comfortable exploring this concept. The children's book *What Are Your Words?* (2021) by Katherine Locke and Anne Passchier offers an age-appropriate introduction to the idea of personal pronouns for four- to eight-year-olds. And the Gender Wheel Curriculum Pronoun Protocol (http://www.genderwheel.com/pronouns/pronoun-protocol/) offers twelve tips to support adults in modeling inclusive language use with children.

> "As with all aspects of a child's development, no two children are exactly alike. The same goes for gender. The more you can read, watch, or listen to the diverse stories of gender-expansive children, the better you'll be able to support all children. And for the times you don't know the 'right answer' or exactly what to do, it never hurts to stop and listen. Children know themselves deeply and are ready to tell us if we can listen with our ears, eyes, hearts, and minds."
>
> —D, father of a 4-year-old transgender daughter and a 2-year-old child

In the next chapter, we'll explore the importance of supporting children in their gender expression and identity development.

IN SUMMARY

Gender is a topic that is relevant and meaningful to all people, regardless of age or experience. Increasing understanding and awareness about terminology, pronouns, gender identity, and development can lead to greater compassion, respect, and connection. Committing to learning more about gender and listening to the perspectives of others can increase your ability to meet children and families where they are.

CHAPTER 2:
THE IMPORTANCE OF AFFIRMATION AND SUPPORT

REDUCING RISKS AND IMPROVING OUTCOMES

Many ECE professionals ask, "Why do we need to make a big deal about this? All kids are welcomed in my classroom. I don't need to make a big deal about gender." Unfortunately, despite the best intentions of adults, children who are gender diverse or expansive are very likely to need specific support to feel safe, welcome, and accepted at school. Both implicit and covert biases are present in nearly every classroom. *Implicit bias* often occurs even when a person is unaware of their bias. They may believe that they do everything possible to not stereotype children or put them into binary gender boxes, but their actions may prove differently. For example, a teacher may state (and even honestly believe!) that they treat all children equally regardless of their gender but may still use gender-normed language to describe actions or behavior, use pink paper to label the girls' cubbies and blue to label the boys', or even subconsciously assume that children will prefer certain activities or future careers based on their perceived gender. *Overt* (also known as *explicit*) *biases* are more obvious and often easier to address, as they are direct. Telling children that they can't use particular toys or materials because of their gender ("The dolls are for the girls!") or using books and songs that emphasize stereotypical gender roles are examples of overt gender bias. While both implicit and explicit gender biases impact all children, children who are gender diverse are particularly susceptible to emotional or other developmental harm from such actions, statements, and beliefs from their care providers.

WHY DO GENDER-DIVERSE CHILDREN NEED SUPPORT?

It's not enough for teachers to say that all children are welcome—we have to make sure that all children *feel* welcome. Because our world is so biased toward a binary gender system, we need to make conscious efforts to ensure that our classrooms are affirming and accepting places for all of the children in our programs.

"I strongly believe in the importance of connection and community. Each student should have a sense of belonging and ownership in the classroom. I want my students to know that who they are matters. That their voice matters. And that they are a unique and special individual who is an essential member of our community.

For me, this work begins right at the first hello. How am I showing my students I am listening? How am I making sure their voices are heard or represented? Am I providing a safe space for them in the classroom? Do they feel comfortable being themselves? I also want to build that sense of community amongst the class, where the teacher and every student has an equal voice. How do we listen to each other? How do we support each other? How do we value what others have to say? What do we do when someone is hurt? How can we work on healing after someone has been hurt? I find self-assessment to be a valuable tool to critique my own practice.

Building a sense of trust and support in the class can take time. But it can be life changing for some students. From my experience, if students do not feel that they are a part of the community, this can be harmful and a block to their growth and learning. I have seen the positive impact that sense of belonging has had on students when they realize they are loved and cared for in their classroom community."

—K, early elementary teacher

HETERONORMATIVITY AND CISNORMATIVITY: A BINARY SOCIETY

We live in a very binary, heteronormative society. As discussed in the previous chapter, adults tend to assign gender to almost everything that children come in contact with. People often make the assumption that people fall into distinct and complementary/opposite genders, roles, expressions, and identities. While there has been growing awareness in education that children often grow up in "nontraditional" families, schools still frequently engage in practices that assume that all children have a mother and a father. Examples of common heteronormative and cisnormative assumptions include having only two gender boxes (M/F) to check on forms or celebrating Mother's Day and Father's Day in the classroom. "Heteronormativity reinforces those identities that conform to 'traditional' expectations of sex, gender, and sexuality, namely, the heterosexual pairing of a biological, cisgender, masculine man and a biological, cisgender, feminine woman" (Bryan, 2012). Due in part to this pervasive cultural emphasis on heteronormativity and binary gender, most gender-expansive children experience feelings of "otherness" or being different, mainly due to the strict societal expectations placed on gender expression.

Young children who do not see themselves or their families reflected in their classrooms are more likely to feel alienated, shameful, or othered. This presents an obstacle to healthy self-esteem and identity development. Families who do not feel acknowledged or welcomed in their children's schools are less likely to be involved and engaged. Additionally, for some gender-expansive children, your classroom may be one of the only places where they feel safe and comfortable exploring who they are. To have the best ECE programs we can, we need to make sure that all of our families and children feel accepted and celebrated.

In chapters 4 and 5, you will find specific suggestions for ways to reduce cis- and heteronormativity in your classrooms and programs.

WHAT DO THE NUMBERS SAY?

The statistics related to children who are gender expansive or transgender can often paint a grim picture for parents and others who care for their children. While most of the data that has been collected to date focuses on transgender teens and young adults, the statistics are frightening. Transgender youth are significantly more likely to exhibit depression, anxiety, and victimization than their cisgender peers. In a large-scale research study released by The Trevor Project in 2019, negative outcomes for transgender teens include one in three attempting suicide.

Gender-expansive children are at risk for multiple mental-health, safety, and developmental concerns when they are reared in an unsupportive or nonaffirming environment. A 2012 study published in *Pediatrics* (Roberts et al.) drew a correlation between gender diversity as a predictor of bullying, abuse, PTSD, depression, and suicide. Luckily, studies show that, when provided with support and affirmation, gender-expansive youth have significantly improved outcomes, better mental health, and development in line with their cisgender peers. A recent study published in the *Journal of the American Medical Association* reports that receipt of gender-affirming care was associated with 60 percent lower odds of moderate or severe depression and 73 percent lower odds of suicidality among a cohort of adolescents (Tordoff,

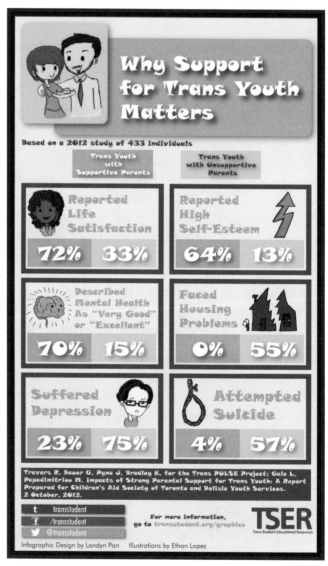

**Source: Trans Student Educational Resources. 2012.
https://transstudent.org/graphics/youthsupport/**

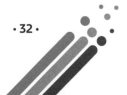

GUIDANCE FOR SUPPORTING **GENDER DIVERSITY** IN EARLY CHILDHOOD EDUCATION

Wanta, and Collin, 2022). *The Report of the U.S. Transgender Survey* indicates that "a chief safety factor in reducing risk is to belong to an accepting family" (2015). All it takes is support! Familial support, especially, can reduce the risk of suicide and substance abuse and can save lives. Anna Bianchi, a social worker, has found that even one supportive adult can make the difference for a child who is gender diverse. "The bottom line is this: where there are allies, there's increasing safety; and where allies are absent, there's increasing risk. Allies, in the stories of gender-expansive children, are a lifeline to increased resilience, healthy self-esteem, and good decision-making capacities" (Bianchi, 2018). While we can't ensure that all the gender-expansive children we work with will have supportive families, we *can* each make sure that our classroom is an affirming and supportive space.

AN AFFIRMATIVE APPROACH

Partially due to the inclusion of gender dysphoria in the *Diagnostic and Statistical Manual of Mental Disorders,* 5th ed. (DSM-5), parents and professionals have often seen gender diversity to be an aberration or mental illness. In the past, it was common for medical professionals to use an extinction approach and tell parents to force their gender-diverse children into strict binary gender roles and expressions. Parents were told to ignore their child's requests for name and pronoun changes, hide or destroy their child's preferred toys and clothing, and provide only those that "matched" the child's assigned gender. They were told to punish children (often physically) for behavior or gender expressions that varied from the norm. This model of treatment did not lead to children authentically embracing their assigned gender identity. On the contrary, there are thousands of heartbreaking case studies and stories of children who felt isolated, unloved, abandoned, and abused. Many gender-expansive children who were "treated" using the extinction model faced trauma and abuse, and some took their own lives. This extinction model advice is still given to parents by some providers today.

REBECCA'S REFLECTION

As parents and educators, we talk frequently with young children about community helpers, especially those who work toward community health and safety—such as teachers, health-care workers, firefighters, and police officers. Our children's interactions with community helpers shape their trust in humanity, their sense of belonging, and their ability to take reasonable risks and try new things. When my son was almost five, we took him into urgent care for stomach pains and fever. The attendant suspected appendicitis and urged us to take him to the large, renowned children's hospital twenty miles away. In the waiting room, I showed my son's insurance card with a sticky note asserting his name and pronouns. We waited in the room for the emergency doctor who entered without knocking and sighed, tipping her head in my son's direction, "So what is it? A boy or a girl?" I did my best in the situation, advocating for my son while trying to avoid any further trauma. But before she left, the physician palpitated his stomach and then looked down his pants, parted his legs and said, "Just checking," before snapping off her gloves and letting me know it was probably the flu. It's been almost three years and he's never forgotten the experience. Up until six months ago, he would still vomit before any type of medical appointment. He still questions me at length beforehand about what will happen and who will look at him.

Luckily, his experience with his teachers has been the opposite. His teachers have been engaged and supportive every year, and school is one of his favorite places. School is where he feels the most autonomy, the most like himself. School is the first place he has gone without me—it's a community that belongs only to him, and like any child, he deserves to feel welcomed and valued in it. He has friends and best friends and brief frenemies and friends again. He has teachers he is safe talking with about anything. His classroom culture is one of kindness, equity, and mutual respect—every child belongs, every child is included, and every child is supported. That is not the case nationwide for trans and gender-diverse children, but it should be. Adults who work with the community, specifically children, and purport to be invested in their health and well-being, must be willing to honor every child's experience.

Luckily, a counterpart to the extinction model emerged. In the past decade, the gender-affirmative approach has become the primary model for children's gender health. In this model, parents and caregivers are encouraged to pay attention to what children tell them about their gender. The affirmative approach allows for acceptance and support by honoring children's preferences for clothing, toys, names, and pronouns. (This approach is outlined in many of the resources shared in appendix A.)

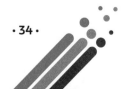

Gender Spectrum, a nonprofit organization with national reach working to create gender-inclusive environments for children, has organized an international consortium of gender-affirmative practitioners. The premises of the gender-affirmative model developed and promoted by this consortium are the following:

- Gender variations are not disorders or pathological.

- Gender variations are healthy expressions of infinite possibilities of human gender.

- Gender presentations are diverse and varied across cultures, requiring cultural sensitivity to those variations.

- Gender involves an interweaving of nature, nurture, and culture.

- A person's gender may be binary or fluid or multiple.

- If people suffer from any kind of emotional or psychiatric problem connected to their gender, this is most likely because of negative reactions to them from the outside world.

- If there is gender pathology, we will find it not in the child, but in the culture (transphobia) (Ehrensaft, 2016).

WHAT IF WE DO NOTHING?

"Why can't we just let them be kids?"

Some adults, while acknowledging that the extinction model is harsh, feel uncomfortable with allowing young children to make choices for their gender expression that are outside the mainstream. They may worry about teasing or bullying and want to protect children from attention and exposure. They may fear that a child is being pushed to choose something they can't understand. Unfortunately, ignoring a child's gender-identity needs can be nearly as harmful as extinction methods. If we do nothing for children who are gender expansive, we are doing something, and what we are doing will lead to harm (Ehrensaft, 2016).

Affirming a child's understanding of who they are is kind, respectful, and responsive. It allows children to explore their own gender identity and determine who they can be. No long-term or lasting negative repercussions have been seen from allowing children to be supported in their gender expression at young ages. In fact, we see only positive outcomes, even when that child's eventual gender identity may shift again. From a developmental perspective, children and teens seldom regret or resent support that they receive, but they commonly resent a lack of support.

When a child tells a trusted adult something about themselves and they are told they are wrong or are ignored, that rejection and invalidation can cause significant developmental issues that can be lifelong. Children need to receive the messages that they can trust how they feel, that they can trust adults to listen to and believe them, and that they can trust themselves.

CREATING A CLASSROOM CULTURE

A CLASSROOM FAMILY

While all children come from unique family cultures, we are able to create the culture of our classroom. As an early childhood educator, and now as a college professor teaching ECE, Jenny has always spoken frequently of the "classroom family." Your classroom family is the result of the values you uphold as the teacher in your classroom. It is the sense that **everyone** in the class feels included and heard. In a family, you stand up for each other, you care about one another (even when you're upset), and you don't kick anyone out. Each new group of children you get as a teacher creates a new classroom family— the dynamics of each individual child and their experiences, culture, and home family influence the classroom family that you will form that year. But as the teacher, you get to set the values and tone for your classroom.

If you work any amount of time with groups of young children, you will have children in your classroom who are gender diverse. Young children are more gender variant and gender fluid (not necessarily trans) than we think. It is important to let children be who they are and not to encourage or pressure them to put names or labels on who they are if they aren't ready for that. Try to avoid putting pressure on children to conform to gender expectations; similarly, avoid pressuring them to be fixed in their gender expression. "[E]ven those of us who are typically gendered do not wear the same clothes every day, and do not like to do the same things every day. The same is true for children. Gender-fluid kids need support in fending off pressures from other people to remain in a more predictable gender state. They need your love and encouragement that they can be just who they are" (Brill and Pepper, 2008).

When we create a classroom culture in which all the members of our classroom family can explore and be who they are on any given day, we create a safe space where children can thrive. When children are given the message that gender is binary, some children feel the need to express themselves as the opposite gender so that they can dress in the clothes they like or play with the toys or friends they prefer. But most gender-diverse children aren't transgender. They simply need a space free from the pressure and constraints of strict gender expectations in order to thrive.

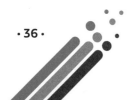

REBECCA'S REFLECTION

When my son was very young, prior to transitioning, he had long rejected any clothes, activities, or accessories that he found to be "girly." Sometimes we would have play dates with large groups of friends, and all the children—boys and girls—would explore the dress-up box, makeup, wigs, and small-heeled plastic princess slippers. Even in those circumstances, he would continue to assert that he would only be a boy in "boy things." He struggled with things he used to enjoy, such as his sister's Barbies and purses, and traded them in for things he found more masculine, such as superheroes and backpacks. When he admired these items in stores, we would remind him that clothes and toys have no gender, and playing or dressing however one is comfortable is all that matters. I used to stand in the aisle between the wide area of the girls' section and the more narrow boys' department in stores. I'd watch him wander with his sister, fingering the mermaid sequin embellishments and soft leggings. Then he'd head to the boy section, looking through the racks of flat graphic tees and thick sweatpants and trousers. Things improved in the years close to 2020, and stores began carrying more gender-neutral clothes that were soft or sparkly. Through kindergarten and first grade, my son stuck firmly to wearing only "boy" clothes. We began to get a lot of hand-me-downs from both boys and girls in the spring/early summer of his first-grade year. I left everything in a big pile for them to go through on their own. My son pulled out a bright yellow jumpsuit, brushed cotton and loose. He told me it was just like what men wore to work on cars. He also pulled out a denim skirt that he'd eventually pair with jeans. "Denim is for everyone, right?" he would check. He started feeling comfortable wearing patterns to school, or loose leggings and surf tees. Red angora cardigans paired with railroad overalls and a baseball cap. He was expressing himself, naturally, finally—modeling what his truest heart liked. Not his gender, not his sex, just what he, at seven, liked.

It was profound to see how rigid our ideas about clothes are, more so than even toys. But it's just fabric, just colors and softness and length and fit we like. My son will occasionally get teased by peers, primarily male, about how he dresses from time to time. But most peers in class seem to admire his confidence and some even echo desires to do the same or express a sudden understanding of how little all those rules about "who wears what" actually matter. His teacher even encouraged us to make a book of people dressed in all sorts of ways. We titled it *Fashion Is for Everyone!* and it lives in their classroom library, where it's pored over frequently, sometimes by a whole group chatting, and sometimes by a singular friend reading through. While no one else in class has expressed a desire to be identified differently and there's been no sudden influx of boys in dresses or girls in pants (see how that sounds?), the children in his class have a better understanding that clothes belong to all of us. There is no wrong way to dress at school.

"As educators, I think we should all be on a path of continuous listening, learning, and improving. We can be a source of knowledge and guidance for parents while also being open to collaboration and discussion. I value feedback and critique immensely because it makes me a better teacher and better person. The parents of our students have valuable insight to share with us because, besides the children themselves, they know them the best. The adults are not the only ones who bring important perspectives. Our students' voices are powerful. They should be listened to and respected, just as much as adult voices. They can have an important role in advocating for themselves if they know they are valued, affirmed, and cared for. Sometimes the support that students need is not acknowledged at home, and the classroom can be a place for them to feel affirmed, safe, and comfortable being themselves."

—K, early elementary teacher

ALLIES

Although you may not be gender creative yourself, you can still be a strong ally for the children and families in your life who are gender diverse. An ally is a person who has committed to unlearning harmful gender stereotypes and misconceptions and is willing to stand up for and with those who are marginalized. In the book *Becoming an Ally to the Gender-Expansive Child* (2018), Anna Bianchi outlines the characteristics of an ally:

- An ally wants to learn.

- An ally strives to be self-aware.

- An ally will work to overcome personal barriers.

- An ally will hold themselves accountable.

- An ally will be child-inclusive.

- An ally will stay stable when things get difficult.

Children can also be powerful allies to their peers and classmates. They often have an easier path to allyship, as they have less "unlearning" to do. But we, as the adults in the ECE program, set the tone and model the expectations for behavior and treatment we value.

FAIRNESS: EQUALITY VS. EQUITY

"It's not fair!" is a refrain commonly heard in ECE classrooms. Young children have a developmental obsession with fairness, and their understanding of the concept is not always accurate. To a young child, fair means equal— everyone gets exactly the same treatment, toy, color of cup, or number of cookies. Unfortunately, many adults also equate fairness with equality.

Equality means that everyone gets the same thing. But *equity* means that everyone gets what they need to be successful. In many situations, equity is more "fair" than equality. If someone is drowning, we want the lifeguard to jump in and save that person, not say, "I can't jump in and save everyone, so I'll save nobody." Saving nobody is equality. Saving the drowning person is equity.

To ensure that **all** the children in our classes and programs feel seen, heard, and understood, we need to strive for equity. Just as a child who is feeling under the weather might need a little extra attention from us, or how we might pay closer attention to the needs of a child whose parents are divorcing, we need to be mindful that children who are gender expansive may need different attention from their teachers.

According to a training by Virtual Lab School called *Creating Gender Safe Spaces*, "Child-development centers and school-age and youth programs have an obligation to create a safe and accepting space for all individuals, including gender-expansive and LGBTQ individuals" (n.d.). As ECE professionals, we should strive to create a space that is equal in that we provide acknowledgement, affirmation, and advocacy for all the children we work with, but that is also equitable in that we recognize that different children will need different types and amounts of acknowledgement, affirmation, and advocacy. For example, a child facing food or housing insecurity may need additional concrete resources from their early childhood program that other children may not need, such as access to clean clothing, to help increase their safety and comfort. A child who is undocumented may benefit from access to resources that a child who is a citizen would not need. A child whose parents are going through a divorce may need more direct attention and affection than a child who is secure at home. The bottom line is that early childhood educators already regularly provide individualized attention and advocacy for the children they work with based on each child's individual needs.

PARENT PERSPECTIVES:
WHAT PARENTS WANT YOU TO KNOW ABOUT SUPPORT

"A teacher's job is to support the growth and well-being of each child."

—J, mother of a 13-year-old transgender son

"I would like adults to know that using the correct pronouns is so affirming to trans youth. It literally takes nothing to support your child, and in return you will get a child who feels loved, supported, and safe."

—A, mother of a 9-year-old transgender son and a 12-year-old cisgender daughter

"I think there is an art to seeing your child for who they are in the moment without pressuring them to decide who they will be forever. I have to fight the urge to ask my daughter to pick her pronouns and declare the flag that fits her best, and, and, and... not because it is trendy or because I am a helicopter parent but because I want to protect her and fight for her to be able to be exactly who she is. I force myself to take the pressure off so that she can do it in her time with my support but not my insistence. I am scared about what the world might do to her and so I make myself available and insert myself when needed."

—J, mother of an 11-year-old gender-diverse daughter and a 13-year-old cisgender son

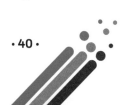

"A few years ago, my adult daughter told me she/they are nonbinary... my response to her was that I loved her and I clearly needed to educate myself so that I could understand her better. I told her it made no difference to me how she identifies, but in truth, even though she's an adult, it does make a difference to a parent. To me the difference was not how I see my child but how others see my child. The thought that she/they might be the subject of ridicule or rejection, that she/they wouldn't be privy to the same considerations in pay or education or even safety, that was heartbreaking. As an early childhood educator, if we have the tools to change an archaic system, it's a responsibility that we can't afford to get wrong."

—C, ECE professional and mother to a nonbinary adult child

"Teachers should strive for allyship—even if this isn't your personal experience it doesn't mean you can't support others."

—M, mother of a 10-year-old gender-creative child, a 12-year-old cisgender son, and a 5-year-old cisgender daughter

"It was horrific to watch my child tank and not be able to get any help from professionals."

—K, mother of a 20-year-old transgender son and an adult cisgender daughter

"Know that every moment can be a struggle for those who are gender variant, so acceptance and understanding is so important."

—H, mother of a 14-year-old transgender son and a 12-year-old cisgender daughter

YOUTH PERSPECTIVES:
WHAT GENDER-DIVERSE KIDS WANT YOU TO KNOW ABOUT SUPPORT

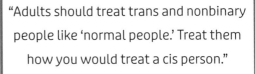

"Adults should treat trans and nonbinary people like 'normal people.' Treat them how you would treat a cis person."

—N, age 9 (he/him/his)

"Being supportive is the most important part. Kids know who they are. You just have to listen."

—X, age 19 (they/them)

"Having friends, both in real life and online, family members, teachers, and health-care providers who were allies even before I came out to them and who made an effort to use the right name and pronouns (and always refer to me as male whenever it was relevant) was crucial. Everyone needs a strong support system and at least one person who'll allow you to live as your true self around them. It's awful to not know anyone who sees you as your actual gender."

—G, college student (he/him)

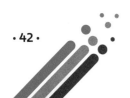

> "Please listen to the child and believe them. They are allowed to [express themselves] and should not be reprimanded nor discouraged if they change their minds. Please give them support and encouragement to explore freely and at their own pace. Use, advocate for, and encourage others to use their correct pronouns. Please support their parents and/or guardians in encouraging them to also support and advocate for their children just as much in this area as they would for their children's scholastic education (if not more)."
>
> **—Chris Mok (he/they)**

> "[When you first meet a child] Just be like 'Hi, hey kid' instead of 'Hey boy' or 'Hey girl' because you don't even know yet. And it doesn't matter anyway."
>
> **—W, age 7 (he/him/his)**

> "What made my transition easy was having supportive friends and teachers. It was easier getting used to my new name and pronouns when they would use them constantly... If a child says that they are transgender, it's important to be respectful and also patient with them. They could always realize later on that their gender identity is actually different, and it's perfectly fine for that to happen—some people won't realize their gender right away and they might keep changing their mind. This doesn't mean that their identity is invalid."
>
> **—R, age 19, (he/him)**

In the next chapter, we'll illustrate how this important work of support, affirmation, and allyship is supported as being part of best practices in our field.

IN SUMMARY

Supporting children in their gender exploration and expression provides an environment in which all children can feel safe, loved, and included. Providing gender-diverse children with support and acceptance can help reduce risks and minimize poor or harmful outcomes, while allowing children to optimally develop their sense of self.

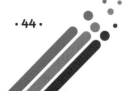

CHAPTER 3:

DEVELOPMENTALLY APPROPRIATE PRACTICE IN EARLY CHILDHOOD EDUCATION: REINFORCEMENT FOR SUPPORTING GENDER DIVERSITY

As ECE professionals, most of us are guided by a true love of and respect for children. The best early childhood teachers and administrators continually work to advance their learning and education, are open to new ideas, and strive to follow best practices as defined by the professional organizations that represent and advocate for ECE. Knowledge, understanding, and science are constantly evolving in our field, requiring ECE professionals to evolve as well.

WHY SHOULD WE SUPPORT GENDER DIVERSITY?

Depending on when you entered the ECE field, gender diversity was likely not a major part of your ECE education and training. But as the cultural and social climate changes, awareness of the need for gender-expansive teaching has increased. While this may be a new topic for some ECE professionals, the data is clear: children who are gender diverse do exist in our programs, and they and their families may have unique needs that we must meet to help them thrive. But we shouldn't just support gender diversity for the children who are gender creative; embracing gender diversity in our ECE programs benefits *all* the children. Recognizing that cisgender assumptions and heteronormativity are pervasive in our society (and in most ECE classrooms), understanding the challenges presented to children as a result are important steps in making meaningful and lasting changes to ECE programs.

Some programs have not addressed gender diversity because they haven't yet felt it to be a need of the children or families in their program. But waiting for an identified gender-diverse child to enter your program to make changes is waiting too long. Instead of treating gender diversity as a problem to be handled, we can embrace gender diversity as a method of making our programs stronger and more well-rounded for children and families. Additionally, if your program has already taken steps to create a more supportive environment for gender expression and creativity, you are creating a program that will be welcoming and embracing for any children who may enter your program in the future. Let's consider the ways that celebrating gender diversity can make your programs stronger and more inclusive for all of your families.

PERSONAL BELIEFS AND BIASES

To begin the work of best supporting gender-diverse children and their families, ECE professionals need to engage in some measure of self-reflection and self-assessment. We are all influenced by our personal experiences, beliefs, and biases—and often our personal assumptions about gender are some of our most deeply held. It can be challenging to engage in the journey

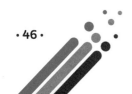

of gender exploration and learning. The first step in helping the children we work with is to discover and reflect on our own personal gender identity and assumptions.

Potential influences on your personal beliefs about gender can include your own gender identity and experiences; your age and generation; your culture, religion, or belief system; your education; the region and area in which you live; your personal relationships with other people; and other factors. Untangling all the potential influences that create complicated feelings about gender identity, particularly in young children, can be difficult work. The importance of self-reflection for teachers as they work to change their practices cannot be underestimated.

Luckily, there are many excellent resources that can assist you in auditing your own beliefs and assumptions as you embark on learning more about gender. One of the best (and most recent), is the book *Supporting Gender Diversity in Early Childhood Classrooms* (2019) written by the team behind Gender Justice in Early Childhood, an advocacy and education organization. Their book (along with the Gender Justice in Early Childhood website, both referenced in appendix A) offers empathetic and powerful tools to assist teachers in the process of self-reflection around gender and early childhood, including classroom-practice audits.

Taking steps and making changes toward a more gender-inclusive classroom and program can only benefit the children you work with. We want our classrooms and ECE programs to be safe spaces for the children we teach. If children feel as though their basic identities are rejected or problematic, they can't feel safe and therefore can't optimally learn and grow. "[I]f teachers are unable to reflect upon their own prejudices, their classrooms are not safe places. If teachers are unwilling to challenge stereotypes, their schools are not inclusive communities. If teachers refuse to see the needs of the children they are responsible for because it is easier not to, then they fail in their professional responsibilities" (Peto, 2011).

As with any journey that involves learning new information and unlearning outdated or incorrect beliefs, this is a process. Learning is ongoing and requires a commitment to be open to new information as it is received. It's not realistic to expect that any ECE program or teacher could make the necessary shifts to a fully inclusive gender-expansive program overnight. Rather, as information is learned and old beliefs are challenged, changes tend to be made incrementally. The important thing is to maintain the goal of inclusion and respect.

THE RELATIONSHIP MODEL

Many early childhood professionals understand the value and importance of what are known as "4R interactions"—interactions with children should be Respectful, Reciprocal, Reflective, and Responsive (Mangione, 2017). Listening and responding to children when they show and tell us who they are is absolutely an example of a 4R interaction. For children to develop optimally and get the most out of their early childhood experience, they need to have strong relationships with the adults who care for them. Positive relationships are the key to learning. As teachers, we can build those relationships and connections in many ways. In *Powerful Interactions: How to Connect with Children to Extend Their Learning*, the authors outline three main steps in optimizing the teacher-child interactions: be present, connect, and extend learning (Dombro, Jablon, and Stetson, 2011). Consider the myriad learning opportunities presented when we engage with children in conversations about gender. As adults, we can ensure that children feel connected to, heard, and valued by the way we interact with them.

The foundation of a high-quality ECE program is respectful and attuned relationships between the adults and the children they care for. Attunement occurs when children feel as though they matter; they feel seen and heard and understood by the adult. Quality teachers know to follow the children's lead, focus on their presence, and engage in positive communication strategies, such as active listening, reflective modeling, and observation. It is optimal for children to be the narrators of their own story rather than being told who they are and what they feel. Imagine the environment that is created when a child is heard, believed, and respected for who they are. That will be an environment in which learning can best take place!

ANTI-BIAS CURRICULUM

Anti-bias education and curriculum encompasses a vision of ECE work in which all children are supported to thrive and flourish and are given the tools to enhance their understanding of others and develop their own self-worth. Louise Derman-Sparks introduced her anti-bias curriculum for ECE in the 1980s. Over the past three decades, multiple books, trainings, workshops, conferences, and resources have been developed under the anti-bias curriculum/education umbrella.

Anti-bias work recognizes that bias and inequities are inherent in the systems in which children develop and strives to minimize or eliminate those inequities in the ECE environment. "It is important to remember that it is not human differences that undermine children's development but rather unfair, hurtful

treatment based upon these differences" (Derman-Sparks and Olsen Edwards, 2010).

As understandings evolve, anti-bias materials are revised. The 2010 edition of the curriculum, *Anti-Bias Education for Young Children and Ourselves* (Derman-Sparks and Olsen Edwards), emphasizes that children should choose their own clothing, interests, and expression; adults should use appropriate and accurate anatomical terminology; and teachers should support expansive gender behavior and model ranges of roles and interests that go beyond gender stereotypes. However, the 2010 edition also instructs teachers to "help preschoolers understand that being a girl or boy depends on how their bodies are made." This is an outdated and binary premise that does not account for the difference between anatomy and gender. Fortunately, the 2020 revised and updated second edition of the curriculum provides a thorough and expansive chapter entirely on gender and gender identity, including promotion of a multifaceted understanding of gender, gender expression, gender identity, gendered language, transgender children, and more. The 2020 edition also highlights the ways that anti-bias education can be applied to gender identity, with specific connection to the goals of the curriculum (Derman-Sparks, Olsen Edwards, and Goins, 2020). The resources, strategies, and information provided in the 2020 edition of *Anti-Bias Education for Young Children and Ourselves* are affirming of children's gender journeys, offer opportunities for self-reflection, and demonstrate the change in understanding related to gender that has occurred over the last decade.

Anti-bias education can be a valuable resource for ECE professionals, offering materials, concepts, research, and frameworks to enhance children's development of self-identity and self-worth. Recognizing the limitations existent in these and many other ECE materials related to gender is an important caution. Because understanding and gender justice issues are evolving at a rapid pace, some otherwise worthy resources can and will be outdated in relation to gender identity. Pay attention to the publication date of materials, and look for resources whose authors show a willingness to update and revise their materials to reflect the most current knowledge and understandings.

POSITION STATEMENTS AND MORE

Many professional organizations, nonprofit advocacy groups, and government entities have issued position and policy statements that provide guidance on working with children who are gender diverse. In the following sections, we review some of the statements that are most relevant to ECE. For the full statements, please visit the websites indicated. Having the reinforcement of position statements from reputable organizations can be helpful for teachers and administrators who want to feel well prepared to respond to any parent questions or concerns about program policies and practices. The statements below are included or mentioned mainly to help support the justification for building gender-supportive ECE programs.

NAEYC POSITION STATEMENTS

The National Association for the Education of Young Children (NAEYC) is the preeminent professional organization for the ECE field. NAEYC standards are seen as markers of quality, and the organization's position statements are supported by current discipline-related studies, data, and science. Many ECE programs work toward NAEYC accreditation, and their research is well regarded in the field. You can learn more about NAEYC at www.naeyc.org. Their five foundational documents are designed to support and reinforce each other in providing guidance for best practices in the ECE field.

The *Professional Standards and Competencies for Early Childhood Educators* (NAEYC, 2019) describes and outlines the six professional standards for the field, providing a nationally recognized basis and professional standard for quality early childhood education.

Gender identity is specifically discussed and referred to in several of the competencies underlying the standards, including the following:

- Competency 1c: "Understand the ways that child development and the learning process occur in multiple contexts, including family, culture, language, community, and early learning setting, as well as in a larger societal context that includes structural inequities" (p. 9).

  A child's developing gender identity is impacted by persistent societal inequities related to gender that can have "long-term effects on children's learning and development" (p. 12).

- Competency 1d: "Use this multidimensional knowledge—that is, knowledge about the developmental period of early childhood, about individual children, and about development and learning in cultural contexts—to make evidence-based decisions that support each child" (p. 9).

- Competency 4c: "Use a broad repertoire of developmentally appropriate, culturally and linguistically relevant, anti-bias, evidence-based teaching skills and strategies that reflect the principles of universal design for learning..." (p. 10).

  "Using the environment and the curriculum to stimulate a wide range of interests and abilities in children of all genders, avoiding the reinforcement of gender stereotypes and countering sexism and gender bias..." (p. 19).

"Incorporating accurate age-appropriate and individually appropriate and relevant information about ethnic, racial, social and economic, gender, language, religious, and LGBTQ+ groups in curriculum and instruction" (p. 19).

- Competency 5c: "Modify teaching practices by applying, expanding, integrating, and updating their content knowledge in the disciplines, their knowledge of curriculum content resources, and their pedagogical content knowledge" (p. 10).

"Early childhood educators encourage and grow every child's interests and abilities in each academic discipline, countering gender, ability, racial, ethnic, and religious biases that can limit children's opportunities and achievements" (p. 23).

The NAEYC professional standards and competencies revolve around the identity of educating the whole child, and gender is clearly a part of that development. "Gender identity is central to development at every age; therefore, it should be addressed if we are attempting to educate the 'whole child'" (Bryan, 2012).

NAEYC's position statement *Developmentally Appropriate Practice* (2020) outlines the guidelines and recommendations for providing developmentally appropriate practice (DAP) in early childhood programs. Gender is included throughout the document as an area of attention for educators to avoid bias and provide equitable learning opportunities. The use of gender-neutral language is highlighted in Principle 7, and gender identity is included in the definitions of diversity and structural inequities.

The *Code of Ethical Conduct and Statement of Commitment* (NAEYC, 2011)

outlines the values and obligations that ECE professionals must be willing to adhere to so they can provide equitable and ethical care. While it can be argued that having respect for all children is perhaps the foundational ethical value of quality ECE care, the statement describes specific standards of behavior that are expected.

Among the core values outlined are several that align directly with the concept of affirming and supportive interactions with and treatment of children who are gender expansive:

- Base our work on knowledge of how children develop and learn

- Respect the dignity, worth, and uniqueness of each individual

- Respect diversity in children, families, and colleagues

- Recognize that children and adults achieve their full potential in the context of relationships that are based on trust and respect (NAEYC, 2011).

Additionally, the following ideals and principles outlined in the code are relevant when considering how to develop practices that are inclusive of children who are gender expansive and their families (NAEYC, 2011):

- Ideal I-1.2: "To base program practices upon current knowledge and research in the field of early childhood education, child development, and related disciplines, as well as on particular knowledge of each child" (p. 2).

- Principle P-1.1: "Above all, we shall not harm children. We shall not participate in practices that are emotionally damaging, physically harmful, disrespectful, degrading, dangerous, exploitative, or intimidating to children. This principle has precedence over all others in this Code" (p. 3).

- Principle P-1.7: "We shall strive to build individual relationships with each child; make individualized adaptations in teaching strategies, learning environments, and curricula; and consult with the family so that each child benefits from the program" (p. 3).

- Ideal I-2.2: "To develop relationships of mutual trust and create partnerships with the families we serve" (p. 3).

- Ideal I-2.4: "To listen to families, acknowledge and build upon their strengths and competencies, and learn from families as we support them in their task of nurturing children (p. 4).

- Ideal 1–2.5: "To respect the dignity and preferences of each family..." (p. 4).

- Ideal I-2.8: "To help family members enhance their understanding of their children, as staff are enhancing their understanding of each child through communications with families..." (p. 4).

- Principle P-2.13: "We shall maintain confidentiality and shall respect the family's right to privacy, refraining from disclosure of confidential information and intrusion into family life" (p. 4).

The position statement *Advancing Equity in Early Childhood Education* (NAEYC, 2019) offers recommendations and support for practices that can

ensure that children are able to develop in an equitable early childhood environment. The statement includes lists of recommendations for both educators and administrators, and should be read in its entirety, as it is very relevant to the themes of this manual. Among other concepts, this position statement states that ECE professionals have a duty to advance equity and help children reach their full potential, highlights the "broader societal context of inequities in which implicit and explicit bias are pervasive" (NAEYC, 2019), and encourages the use of inclusive teaching strategies to show children that they are valued and important. Gender is specifically referred to throughout the position statement, including multiple references to "all genders," showing an awareness of the gender spectrum.

The article "Embracing Equity: Helping All Children Reach Their Full Potential" (Allvin, 2018) discusses NAEYC's support for equity and awareness: "NAEYC is for the active embrace of equity. We are for talking openly and honestly about diversity, and we are for changing our policies and practices to enhance our organizational commitment to being high performing and inclusive. We are for living these core values and beliefs:

- Recognize that children are best understood and supported in the context of family, culture, community, and society.

- Respect the dignity, worth, and uniqueness of each individual (child, family member, and colleague).

- Respect diversity in children, families, and colleagues.

- Recognize that children and adults achieve their full potential in the context of relationships that are based on trust and respect.

- Advocate for policies, practices, and systems that promote full and inclusive participation.

- Confront biases that create barriers and limit the potential of children, families, and early childhood professionals" (Allvin, 2018).

CALIFORNIA HEALTH EDUCATION FRAMEWORK

Issued by the California Department of Education (CDE), "curriculum frameworks provide guidance to educators, parents, and publishers, to support implementing California content standards" (CDE, 2016). The California Health Education Framework states that "dispelling myths about gender expectations in kindergarten can lay the groundwork for acceptance, inclusiveness, and an anti-bullying environment in schools" (CDE, 2019). Chapter 3 of the Health Education Framework, "Transitional Kindergarten through Grade Three" specifically addresses gender identity and expression:

Students also learn about individual differences, including gender, from a very early age. Gender socialization begins before children start school—students may believe that different norms are associated with people of particular genders by the time they enter kindergarten. While this understanding may be limited, students can still begin to challenge gender stereotypes in a way that is age appropriate. While students may not fully understand the concepts of gender expression and identity, some children in kindergarten and even younger have identified as transgender or understand they have a gender identity that is different from their sex assigned at birth. The goal is not to cause confusion about the gender of the child but to develop an awareness that other expressions exist. This may present itself in different ways including dress, activity preferences, experimenting with dramatic play, and feeling uncomfortable self-identifying with their sex assigned at birth. However, gender nonconformity does not necessarily indicate that an individual is transgender, and all forms of gender expression should be respected" (CDE, 2019).

K-12 SEXUALITY AND HEALTH EDUCATION GUIDELINES

Some states (in addition to California) include gender diversity, identity, and roles in their state curriculum guidelines for health and sexuality education. For example, Oregon includes gender identity in the health education provided to all grade levels: "Many children start expressing their gender identity in early childhood, and it is the responsibility of public education to provide safe places for all students, regardless of their gender expression or identity, so they can learn and grow" (Oregon Department of Education, n.d.). The District of Columbia Health Education Learning Standards require that schools provide a comprehensive and age-appropriate curriculum that supports the importance of gender identity and expression. Other states include similar requirements in their health education standards.

A Call to Action: LGBTQ+ Youth Need Inclusive Sex Education (SEICUS et al., 2021), a joint report from ten advocacy and education organizations, highlights the status of health education in the United States. According to the report, only twenty-nine states and the District of Columbia require that sexuality education be taught in the public school system, and only six states and DC require LGBTQ+ inclusive sexuality education. Other states ban LGBTQ+ inclusive education or require that teachers frame such identities and relationships in outwardly negative ways (SIECUS et al., 2021).

NATIONAL ASSOCIATION OF SCHOOL PSYCHOLOGISTS (NASP) POSITION STATEMENTS

The *Safe Schools for Transgender and Gender Diverse Students* (NASP, 2014) position statement affirms that gender diversity and transgender identity are not disorders and that gender-diverse and transgender children need safe and supportive school environments. The statement outlines standards of practice for school psychologists, including advocating for the rights of the transgender or gender-diverse student, fostering a climate of acceptance and keeping a child's gender identity and assignment at birth within the child's control to disclose or release.

A joint resolution from the American Psychological Association and NASP (2015), *Resolution on Gender and Sexual Orientation Diversity in Children and Adolescents in Schools,* outlines research and data about gender-diverse children and resolves that affirming, supportive interactions and advocacy are of primary importance in ensuring healthy development.

AMERICAN ACADEMY OF PEDIATRICS POLICY STATEMENTS

The AAP policy statement "Ensuring Comprehensive Care and Support for Transgender and Gender-Diverse Children and Adolescents" outlines specific challenges faced by gender-diverse children and their families and offers "suggestions for pediatric providers that are focused on promoting the health and positive development of youth that identify as TGD [transgender and gender diverse] while eliminating discrimination and stigma" (Rafferty et al., 2018).

It is important to note that throughout the policy statement, gender-affirmative care is held up as the standard, and care providers are cautioned against providing care that can contradict a child's gender identity.

Published in conjunction with the Human Rights Campaign, *Supporting and Caring for Transgender Children* (Murchison et al., 2016) is a policy statement and guiding document that offers a comprehensive view of gender diversity in childhood and supports a gender-affirmative model of care.

AMERICAN CIVIL LIBERTIES UNION (ACLU)

Schools in Transition: A Guide for Supporting Transgender Students in K–12 Schools is a guide for school staff produced by the ACLU, Gender Spectrum, the Human Rights Campaign Foundation, the National Education Association, and the National Center for Lesbian Rights. The information covered is comprehensive. The guide states that "looking at the process of supporting transgender students holistically, everything boils down to the basic principle that students can and should be supported and able to attend schools where their authentic gender is recognized and honored" (Orr et al., n.d.).

AMERICAN PSYCHOLOGICAL ASSOCIATION (APA)

"How Educators Can Support Families with Gender Diverse and Sexual Minority Youth: Promoting Resiliency for Gender Diverse and Sexual Minority Students in Schools" (APA, n.d.) highlights the importance of family and school support for children who are gender diverse. It includes tips, resources, and references.

HUMAN RIGHTS CAMPAIGN

Supporting and Caring for Our Gender Expansive Youth: Lessons from the Human Rights Campaign's Youth Survey (Baum et al., n.d.) is an extensive, easy-to-read, and well-designed report summarizing the findings from a large-scale survey of gender-expansive youth. It includes recommendations for caregivers and parents as well as strategies for teachers in best supporting children. The overarching theme is that children have the best outcomes when they are supported and affirmed in their gender identity.

IN SUMMARY

The information contained in the listed policy and position statements is valuable only if it is applied by teachers and care providers. While policy statements do not offer all the information needed to develop best practices, they can be useful support for the policies you develop for your classrooms and programs.

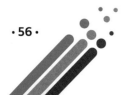

CHAPTER 4:
THE ROLE OF THE EARLY CHILD-HOOD TEACHER

Early childhood classroom teachers, aides, and support staff work as a team with the administrators of their program. You are encouraged to also read and utilize the strategies outlined in Chapter 5: The Role of the ECE Administrator to supplement the information in this section.

> "The preschool we ended up enrolling our children in was one our daughter had previously attended a few years prior to her social transition. The staff had recently been trained by a professional in the field on how to create an inclusive space for gender-expansive children and were outwardly supportive. They also took small steps, such as creating more privacy in the bathroom by adding a curtain at the door. There were a

few issues with staff and peers misgendering/dead-naming*
our daughter; however, these seemed to improve quickly,
and staff always corrected themselves. At times it was also a
struggle to get staff to understand how our daughter's very
recent transition might impact her overall behavior in the
classroom. I'm not sure they recognized the cumulative effects
of microaggressions such as dead-naming. I wonder if greater
knowledge, training, and understanding might have helped the
staff be able to support our daughter more fully."

—D, father of a 4-year-old transgender daughter

*Authors' note: *Dead name* is a term used to refer to a person's
name given at birth that they no longer use because it does not
conform to their gender identity. Dead-naming is considered an
aggressive act when done intentionally or repeatedly.

TIPS FOR EARLY CHILDHOOD EDUCATORS

The average ECE classroom teacher spends thirty-five hours a week with their
students. ECE caregivers are uniquely positioned to make a real difference in
the lives of children, and a positive and supportive school or care environment
can help enhance children's development and resiliency. As an ECE teacher,
you can build strong connections with the children in your classes and their
families by creating a welcoming and inclusive classroom and curriculum.
Many strategies can help you remove gender stereotypes from your teaching
and ensure that all children feel as though they are a valued part of your
classroom.

MONITORING REACTIONARY BIAS

As discussed in the previous section, our own biases, beliefs, and
preconceptions influence how we respond to gender diversity. Early childhood
educators affect gender-identity development by maintaining particular
expectations of children based on their perceived gender, potentially
limiting certain play or by encouraging certain behavior. This is typically
subconscious—most teachers would say that they are not biased about
children's gender expression, but the reality is that nearly all adults are biased
and show that bias in covert and overt ways.

When working with young children, it's valuable to build awareness of your
own reactions, both verbal and nonverbal. Often our facial expressions can
express judgment, even if we are not verbally giving feedback to a child.
Young children are very perceptive and pick up on what the adults around

them want from them. Be careful about how your reactions to a child's dress, play, behavior, or expression could unintentionally influence a child's choices. According to a training by Virtual Lab School called "Creating Gender Safe Spaces," even when children are not directly reprimanded, they frequently get the message that they are wrong for liking certain toys or clothing or that they need to keep certain preferences hidden. Because we are such important influences on children's choices, we may need to take extra care to remain neutral when children are expressing themselves in ways that are nontraditional or nonbinary. Your personal beliefs should not interfere with your ability to provide an inclusive classroom for the children you work with.

Pairing with a coworker to provide observation feedback can be a helpful tool in increasing mindfulness about our reactions to children's gender expressions. Take turns visiting each other's classrooms and paying attention to adult interactions with the children. Such feedback can be valuable in helping highlight areas for work on your teaching, classroom arrangement, or interactions with the children that you may not notice yourself.

GENDER-NEUTRAL LANGUAGE

As discussed in chapter 1, the language we use is important. Adjusting your language to be less gendered and more gender neutral can have a powerful effect in creating an inclusive environment and helping all children feel important and recognized. *Gender-neutral language* (GNL) refers to attempts to remove binary gender systems or gender assumptions from our referential language. We cannot always know someone's gender unless they tell us, thus the attempt to refrain from using gendered references can help ensure that we don't unintentionally exclude or offend. Some of these changes are simple, and others take effort to break long-standing linguistic habits. For example, Jenny used to frequently use the phrase "you guys" or *guys* to refer to groups, but she is now mindful to self-correct and adjust to using terms such as *y'all* or *everyone* instead. While Jenny, as a cisgender woman, doesn't personally mind being referred to as *dude* or a part of *guys*, she recognizes that this isn't true for everyone. Making changes such as referring to the *children* instead of "boys and girls" is one simple switch that can help create a classroom that is welcoming to all. Other classroom-appropriate words and phrases to replace "boys and girls" include *class*, "my friends," "Room 4," *preschoolers*, or simply *everyone*. Some teachers prefer to refer to a child's *grownups* or *adults* rather than *parents* or "mom and dad."

> "I work at a preschool, and we did a brief overview on ways to be more gender inclusive in our staff meeting today: gender-neutral terms, splitting the class by shirt color or the favorite of two animals or foods, or by counting 1, 2, etc. instead of

using boy/girl. We also discussed using singular *they* and the importance of not being 'gender detectives,' etc."

—V, ECE professional and mother of a 6-year-old transgender daughter and a 3-year-old cisgender son

Another step in using GNL is to use people's names to refer to them rather than a gendered reference. It is good practice in our classrooms to refer to children by their preferred name whenever possible and to avoid using diminutives such as *sweetie* or *honey* or using *dude*, which can feel gendered to the subject. And remember, it doesn't hurt anyone to use a name that a child prefers—for some children it's a short-lived phase ("Call me Spider-Man!") associated with their cognitive and social-emotional development, and for other children who may be transgender or gender expansive, it can be a search for comfort and identity. Please don't persist in using a child's birth name if they have shown discomfort or become upset when referred to by that name.

INSTEAD OF		TRY
his/hers	→	theirs
boys/girls	→	children/class
men/women	→	everyone/people
lady/man	→	person
ladies/gentlemen	→	honored guests
mother/father	→	parents/guardians
wife/husband	→	spouse/partner
brother/sister	→	sibling
son/daughter	→	child
guys	→	everyone/folks/y'all

Consider other ways in which you might use gender to influence your language. Many adults frequently comment on girls' appearance ("I love your pretty dress!") and comment on boys' actions and abilities ("You are so fast

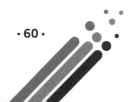

when you run!"). Try to adjust your feedback and focus on all children's skills and qualities ("You were so kind to save a seat for Ryan!") to avoid gendered compliments. Describing children's behavior rather than labeling is another strategy that avoids gender expectations (National Center on Parent, Family, and Community Engagement, n.d.).

> "I usually hear someone mentioning an action because of the sex of the child. "Bobby is so gentle for a boy," or "Jolee is so tough for a girl." I personally make it a point to show appreciation for all emotions in all children: Bobby gets praised for being human and having human emotions and human reactions to things, and so does Jolee."
>
> —S, toddler lead teacher

A variety of ways enable you to adjust your language to increase inclusion, not just in relation to gender but in terms of ability, physical appearance, and behaviors. As you make adjustments to include more GNL in your vocabulary, you may find that you are becoming more aware of other areas in which to make adjustments to your language use as well.

GROUPING WITHOUT GENDER

More than almost any other classroom feature, grouping of children is mentioned by gender-diverse people and their parents as being one of the most impactful. In a typical ECE or K–12 classroom, children are grouped multiple times throughout the school day—to line up, to sit at tables, to form smaller groups for work, to be excused for handwashing or restroom use, and more. And one of the most common methods is to group boys and girls separately. This can unintentionally create extremely difficult and uncomfortable situations for gender-diverse children. Children who feel as

though they "fit" better in the other group, or children who feel as though they don't fit in either group are forced to make a choice that can feel painful, stressful, or impossible. Luckily, this is an easy area to make changes to help all children feel more comfortable. And using varied methods of grouping children offers ECE teachers great opportunities for concrete skill building.

Instead of grouping children by gender, try grouping children in nongendered ways. This approach will allow you to simultaneously build developmentally appropriate skills while practicing classroom management. Ideas include grouping children by:

- shirt or clothing color,

- birth month,

- the first letter of their first (or last) name,

- hair or eye color,

- favorite snack (offer as many options as there are groups), and

- counting off.

Similarly, avoid requesting volunteers or calling for helpers using gender ("I need two boys and one girl") and instead use other descriptors. The goal in our classrooms should be to avoid separating children along gender lines and avoid calling children out based on gender. Adults tend to use gender frequently to label children ("Look at that boy playing over there.") and while usually not purposeful or even meaningful, this type of labeling only helps reinforce to children that gender is very important (Spears Brown, 2014). Families can also be encouraged to avoid birthday-party or playdate invitations based on gender. Help families see how their children play and build relationships across gender lines. Separating children by gender also helps emphasize an "us versus them" mentality that can contribute to children being averse to interaction with other genders. Instead, let's work on ways we can help children see each other for more than just their gender.

"PLAY IS FOR EVERYONE": SETTING CLASSROOM RULES AND COMMUNICATION

Among their many roles, ECE teachers create the guidelines and standards for the classroom and communicate effectively with the children and families. In addition to the following tips, communication with families is covered in chapter 6.

In general, using active listening techniques will go a long way toward helping children feel welcomed and safe in your classroom. Instead of correcting children ("No, you're a boy," or "Girls pee sitting down"), try responding to a child's assertion by saying, "Tell me more." Often children can express what

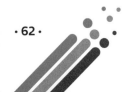

they need from us if we are willing to hear them. Using descriptive statements such as, "You are upset that Joey called you a girl," are often more productive than offering your own opinions or judgments about situations or feelings and can lead to richer conversations and deeper understanding.

When discussing gender, try to avoid using absolutes such as "all girls…" or "all boys…" Instead, discuss patterns using words such as *some*, *most*, or *many*. For example, "Many boys have short hair. Some boys have long hair." In this way, you can help children understand the difference between rules and patterns. Remember, gender is such a vast spectrum that there is no *all* in gender!

RESPECT

It's important that classroom teachers set the expectation that respect is important and goes all ways. Classroom rules in an ECE classroom boil down to three main guidelines: respect yourself, respect others, and respect the environment (or be kind, be safe, be neat). We want to model respect in addition to expecting it, and we want the children to respect others while feeling secure in the expectation that they will also be respected. It is reasonable to insist that the children in your class are treated with respect by their peers, other adults, and yourself.

One way to respect children is to honor their requests about names and pronouns and as well as how they describe and refer to themselves. Another way to show respect is to help children see, through your continued words and actions, that you will keep your classroom safe for *all* the children. This will mean helping children develop kind conflict-resolution skills, stepping in when necessary, and being mindful of how all the children are feeling.

KIND CORRECTION AND CONFRONTATION

Young children are developmentally very rule-bound in many ways. They commonly call out behavior or actions that seem to disrupt expected categorization. Children are also extremely observant and point out differences. These characteristics can combine to make for uncomfortable situations for adults who need to help children navigate interactions with others. The ECE teacher can provide kind language for children to use in their descriptions and help disrupt unkind behavior or gender stereotypes when they show up in the classroom.

Although it can be tempting to ignore gender-confining statements ("Only girls play with dolls") or potentially awkward observations ("Sam is sitting down to pee"), it's important to correct misconceptions in the moment. Show the children and families that your classroom is a place where people can express their gender however they see fit and that gender stereotypes have no place.

Responding matter-of-factly and kindly ("All children can play with the dolls") can model statements that children can use in the future. Recognize that views on and messages about gender affect all the children in your class, not just those who are gender expansive (Virtual Lab School, n.d.). Sending the message that there are no "girl" things or "boy" things and that all children can enjoy everything in your classroom will help create a safe and nurturing environment where children can thrive emotionally and developmentally.

> "I think it is important to develop a sense of community and trust among the students and the teachers. That way, when issues of teasing or bullying come up, they can be safely reported and addressed. A few years ago, two older students teased a younger student for having nail polish on. I addressed it with the individual students and families of the children who did the teasing, but then I also included the topic in our class community discussion time. When issues arise, I think it is important to include the general topic in our class discussions (without naming names and as long as it maintains students' privacy), so it can be a learning opportunity for the class as a whole."
>
> —C, preschool teacher

Avoid the urge to redirect questions or conversation about gender and gender identity. Doing so sends a strong message to children that those ideas and topics are inappropriate or make adults uncomfortable. Instead, use those questions and statements to lead you toward deeper conversation or to use children's books to explore the ideas.

USING CHILDREN'S BOOKS EFFECTIVELY

Picture books are an integral part of the ECE environment. Engaging children in books and stories is key for optimal development, and most ECE classrooms use books during large-group times, as well as for small-group and one-on-one interactions. Curating the books that are always available to children in the classroom library, as well as carefully choosing books to share with the large group during circle time, are important parts of daily planning. Books provide opportunities for conversation starters, allow children to be exposed to new ideas and to see themselves and their families reflected in the larger world, and offer entries to pretend and social play.

As part of making your classroom more gender inclusive, taking a careful review of your classroom library will be an important first step. Even if you don't feel ready to actively introduce gender conversations, you can begin to

diversify your classroom library. Take a look at the books that are available to your students. Pay attention to their covert and overt messages about gender and gender roles—some books will have those topics as a main theme or plot device. Other books are about general or varied topics but have characters or images that portray diverse gender expression or roles. Both types of books are important!

Notice the gender stereotypes that may be present in books you currently have in your library—are these books necessary or can they be removed? Look for books with gender-neutral protagonists and books that disrupt gender stereotypes. Do you have books that portray diverse family structures and gender roles?

When you are reading books to children, ask the question, "What do you notice?" when you are discussing illustrations or plot. Children will point out features of the story and characters that resonate with them, allowing you to tune in to what they notice and find important. Avoid judgment or labeling; use open-ended questions to help children navigate the stories.

Another simple thing you can do to diversify gender portrayals in children's books is to change pronouns when reading stories (even between readings). Often children's books feature animals, monsters, or other fantasy creatures. Change the pronouns that are used and see how children react. If they insist, for example, that a character is a girl, ask why. These sorts of conversations can help you understand what the children see as being gender markers and can open the door to great conversations about colors, clothing, toys, and behaviors belonging to all genders.

When you are reading a book or singing a song that is a staple in your classroom repertoire, you may notice gender stereotypes or binary/heteronormative characterizations that you were previously oblivious to. You can interrupt your reading or singing to address those stereotypes and ask the children how they could change the lyrics or the story to be more inclusive. You may also need to confront and refute stereotypes or bias that are present, especially in classic texts.

While all ECE classrooms can benefit from including more gender-diverse children's books in the classroom library, it's particularly important to include books with gender-diverse characters and themes if you have children in your class who are (or who have family members who are) gender expansive. Children need to see themselves reflected in their classroom, and they may be reassured by or have questions that can be answered by books in the classroom library.

Appendix A offers suggestions for many children's books that might be appropriate additions to your classroom library, including several book lists and other resources. Literature and stories are a vital part of a rich ECE experience, and we can use them to create more inclusivity and diversity in our classrooms and in our student's lives.

LESSON PLANNING WITH GENDER IN MIND

In addition to the books you use in your classroom, you can incorporate gender diversity into many areas and aspects of your planning. In the planning cycle, teachers start by observing the children and move toward brainstorming, choosing activities, gathering materials and supplies, implementing the activities, and observing the children engage, and then they start the cycle over again. Teachers may notice that children are engaging in pretend play that mirrors themes and stories from the books you share, or their play may start to incorporate some of the conversations about gender you may be having as a class.

> "In the various classrooms I have taught in, gender roles tend to be one of the most persistent stereotypes I have addressed. Sports teams, clothing colors and styles, bathrooms, hairstyles, and television and movie characters are just some of the ways children are exposed to gender roles at a young age. This has been an area for me where I am continuing to seek more resources and support as I decide how best to rework stereotypes such as, "Pink is a girl's color." We have had many class conversations and read books but there still seems to be a need for continued conversation. I think one of the best ways to eradicate some of these stereotypes is for children to see numerous real-world examples that contradict what they believe to be true."
>
> —K, early elementary teacher

You do not need to plan only activities that are specifically gender diverse. Rather, you can make small adjustments to your typical planning for each learning area in your classroom that will allow more gender-expansive play and exploration to take place. For example, pay attention to the areas of your classroom and which children tend to spend their time in which area. You may notice gender-segregated patterns in the different learning areas. If you are finding that girls are avoiding the block area or boys are seldom in the dramatic-play space, or if you are noticing patterns for individual children, you can work on developing plans that incorporate materials or themes for those

areas that would attract different children. Make sure that your housekeeping area and dramatic-play area include costumes and props that appeal to all children and are not gender segregated. For example, if you only have pink aprons and high heels in the dress-up area, you may be contributing to unintentional gender stereotypes about play. Often you can meld and mix learning spaces in your classroom to encourage mixing of children.

Try putting materials and toys in different areas of the room. Use dolls or stuffed animals in the block area as an invitation to play. Consider moving areas of your classroom outdoors during outside play time. For example, many children who avoid painting inside are drawn to the easels when they have an opportunity to paint in the sun.

> "When the classroom is set up in a way that materials may leave their designated sections, or when traditionally gender-biased toys are placed in the opposite centers, then play will be encouraged for all. Place blocks in or next to the toy kitchen—the blocks can be used as make-believe materials and can be used to build structures. Children can use those few blocks to expand their play, giving time and exposure to new learning centers."
>
> —E, ECE lead teacher

Consider inviting guests to your classroom to speak about different careers or community roles, and pay attention to inviting people who are subverting gender stereotypes. Don't be afraid to consider inviting gender-diverse people to your classroom, as long as your area and school climate provide a safe space for you and your guests. Creating a welcoming environment can be done without politicizing your classroom space.

Another aspect of planning to be mindful of is ensuring that your classroom activities and circle activities are free from gender stereotypes. Avoid talking about girls being mommies and boys being daddies; you can talk about children being parents instead. Make sure that families are included in ways that are meaningful. Don't assume that only mothers can volunteer in your classroom or that all dads work full-time.

"Creating Gender Safe Spaces," a training from Virtual Lab School, presents many ideas for lesson planning that are gender inclusive. One such idea, the Stereotype Game, comes from author Laurel A. Dykstra and could be appropriate in the preschool classroom:

> Teach kids what a stereotype is (e.g., monsters are scary, boys are noisy, girls like dolls), and ask children to identify

stereotypes in their play, in your teaching, in books, and in advertisements. This skill is helpful not only for making a safe space for gender-expansive and LGBTQ children and youth, but it also helps all children be careful thinkers about the messages in their environments. This website provides more information on stereotypes in children's media exposure and how this affects children's development: https://www. commonsensemedia.org/research/watching-gender. By talking about stereotypes, you can help prevent some of the negative consequences of stereotypes read or seen in different forms of media (Virtual Lab School, n.d.).

CLASSROOM ENVIRONMENTAL ARRANGEMENT

The way you set up your classroom and arrange your materials is a big contributor toward how children feel engaged or welcomed to various activities. Classroom decor and visual cues can be adjusted to be more gender inclusive and less segregated. For example, consider cubby labels. In many classrooms, the children's cubbies are labeled with their names and photos. Do you use different colors or fonts for girl labels and boy labels? If so, consider making them a uniform style instead.

> "The topic of gender-specific colors came up a few times this past year in the classroom. One student was persistent with the idea that pink was a girls' color. It took many individual conversations and class discussions about colors before this misconception started to shift. The class and I talked about making a class book about how colors are for everyone."
>
> —S, early elementary teacher

Think about providing dramatic play props that cross gender lines, and offer costumes and materials in a variety of colors. Having pink hard hats in addition to yellow ones and black skirts in addition to purple ones will help children feel comfortable trying new roles or play.

> "Years ago, I had a boy, Jonny, in my class who would stare at the girls in long dresses. I asked if he wanted to play, but he always said no. But he wouldn't play anything else. One day I picked up a big dress, got close to him, and said, 'This will fit you perfectly!' His eyes got wide and he smiled. Another child

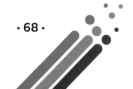

overheard and laughed, so I looked at the child who laughed and said, 'Those are clothes. If you don't want to try it, you do not have to, but Jonny and I are going to have fun.' A third boy heard me and decided he wanted to wear a dress as well. For the next few days, I had boys taking turns to wear the dresses; even the child who initially made fun took turns wearing a dress. I took really good pictures. Unfortunately I never had the strength to share the pictures with the parents or to even talk about it with anybody else."

—M, preschool lead teacher

In their article "Tate and the Pink Coat," the authors suggest selecting "materials that invite exploration without imposing gender expectations" (Kroeger, Recker, and Gunn, 2019). They recommend neutral color palettes and open-ended materials, such as fabric instead of premade costumes. The idea is not to eliminate gender from the classroom but rather to give children the tools they need to express gender in a variety of ways. We want children to feel invited and encouraged to use materials, not excluded or embarrassed.

CLASSROOM MANAGEMENT

In addition to the suggestions about grouping children without using gender, you can also make sure that your other classroom-management practices are more inclusive. Avoid stereotyping classroom responsibilities. There should not be "girl" jobs and "boy" jobs. Similarly, make sure you aren't inadvertently promoting stereotypical gender roles by only asking the boys to help you carry things, for example. Challenge put-downs that might be occurring related to gender, and reflect on how you use language that could be contributing to the idea that certain genders are preferable for certain tasks, responsibilities, or games.

Make sure that you are not segregating by gender using color or other markers; all children should have access to the same colors of materials and classroom furnishings. Remember, things, colors, jobs, feelings, clothes, behaviors, and toys do not belong to any particular gender. Avoiding binary classroom management practices will help all your students feel as though they are recognized and important.

CELEBRATING ALL CHILDREN

All the children in our classrooms are valuable members of our classroom family, and all children deserve to be celebrated. Using a child-centered approach in which you consider the needs and interests of the child, as determined by the child themself, helps ensure that each child is placed at the center of your program and planning. When we are advancing on our own learning journey toward gender inclusion, it is easy to let our enthusiasm for

PARENT PERSPECTIVES:
WHAT PARENTS WANT YOU TO KNOW ABOUT GENDER DIVERSITY IN ECE

"L had great experiences in preschool. He presented as masculine but still had his female birth pronouns and name. His preschool affirmed him and went with it when he would assert he was a boy. I particularly appreciated that the school stayed fluid and open."

—J, mother of a 13-year-old transgender son

"Teachers should understand inclusive versus exclusive language—don't leave out anyone in your language. Teachers should strive for allyship. Even if this isn't your personal experience, that doesn't mean you can't support others. Give children the opportunity to express themselves in any way. Don't put them in a box."

—M, mother of a 10-year-old gender-creative child, a 12-year-old cisgender son, and a 5-year-old cisgender daughter

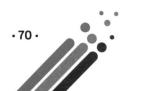

celebrating a child whom we want to support overwhelm or tokenize that child. Avoid expecting that gender-diverse children in your class will serve as examples or will teach the other children. All children deserve to be children, and all children deserve to be simultaneously celebrated for their uniqueness while also being treated as one of the group. Everyone is an expert on their own life and identity. It's important to allow children to express their gender identity without trying to change, punish, or highlight them.

"We feel so lucky that G's daycare and preschool were very supportive of her preferences. Teachers need to respect how children feel. It's important not to separate or group children based on their perceived gender."

—K, mother of an 18-year-old transgender daughter

"Not separating the children by gender is so important. We appreciated that [our son's] preschool did not point out differences or make [him] feel singled out."

—H, mother of a 14-year-old transgender son and a 12-year-old cisgender daughter

"The biggest thing for me is about the shame kids are made to feel if they choose something labeled 'untraditional.' The second thing is the pressure from peers and teachers to follow what others that 'look like them' are doing. We look for playtime and [classroom] areas to be without gender. We look for books and coloring books that offer all kinds of diversity within them. We look for images within the classroom."

—A, trans father of a toddler

"They just let E be E, at whatever place he-then-she showed up. They did a great job answering questions from curious classmates, 'Is E a boy or a girl?' 'Why does E wear dresses if he's a boy?' or nipped in the bud any inklings of teasing. They read age-appropriate books to the class about gender diversity. They also did a good job keeping us (her parents) in the loop about what things E was saying or expressing at school, so that we could track what her gender expression was like at home versus school."

—C, mother of a 7-year-old transgender daughter and a 9-year-old cisgender son

"Because early childhood education is so formative, teachers really need to constantly discuss everyone's differences and treating each other with kindness."

—K, mother of a 13-year-old transgender daughter

"[An ideal preschool would have] genderless single-stall bathrooms, genderless instruction, and pairing children outside gender expression more often, like forcing children out of single-gender groupings. There should also be lots of different kinds of books, aiming on the side of diversity versus normative representations while avoiding token representation."

—R, mother of a 7-year-old transgender son and 9-year-old cisgender daughter

"1. Take gender completely out of everything. No more "boys and girls." Young children get shut down when forced to choose when they don't identify easily in a box. We don't want them to have to make decisions rather than be who they are. There is not a lot of awareness that there may be people who identify as neither or both or in between. We don't want children to bury their true identity. 2. Open up opportunities for play and interaction and environment for all students. 3. As an educator, take the time to overcome personal bias. It's not about changing your personal beliefs and values but about serving all children. Check your personal beliefs at the door to do your job."

—K, mother of a 20-year-old transgender son and an adult cisgender daughter

"I appreciated that the staff had training in this area prior to us even enrolling. It helped that it wasn't centering on our child but rather a way to support all children better. I do wish the staff were better prepared to understand how gender expansiveness, social transitions, and microaggressions can impact a child globally. It's not as simple as using the right pronouns or saying, 'All kids can wear dresses.'"

—D, father of a 4-year-old transgender daughter and a 2-year-old child

YOUTH PERSPECTIVES: WHAT GENDER-DIVERSE KIDS WANT YOU TO KNOW ABOUT GENDER DIVERSITY IN ECE

> "I just wish I could ask them [teachers] to let kids try things out. If they want to dress up as a gender other than their assigned one or be referred to as that, let them experiment. If that kid is cis, then they will just be able to not do that. If that kid is trans, it might help them feel more comfortable and figure themselves out a lot sooner."
>
> **—L, age 15 (she/they/fae)**

EDUCATOR PERSPECTIVES: WHAT ECE PROFESSIONALS WANT YOU TO KNOW ABOUT GENDER DIVERSITY IN ECE

> "The classroom culture I try to instill is that everyone gets to decide what is right for themselves. And we can't decide what is right for someone else. We all get to decide what we want to wear, what we like to do, and who our friends are. The goal is for all students to feel comfortable being themselves and to feel safe and supported in their classroom community."
>
> **—K, early elementary teacher**

"I think they [teachers] should talk more about feelings. Because if we knew everybody's feelings we could get along better."

—W, age 7 (he/him/his)

"Teach them about gender identity, expression, and just like biology in general... they should wear what they want, and if they want to experiment with names and pronouns, let them. Like I wish I knew about transgender being a thing so I didn't have to figure it out alone, that it's okay not to know who you are—take your time figuring yourself out. That clothes really have no gender, they can wear what they want; at the end of the day it's just cloth. One thing I didn't hear enough is that if you think you are trans but you like some things that are stereotypical with your birth sex, that's okay."

—W, age 17 (he/him)

"Often a boy will hesitate to play with dolls or choose the color pink because it's a 'girl activity,' and vice versa. If the stereotypes and gender attachments are removed, the children are empowered to choose freely, without feeling admonished by their peers by going against the grain of gender norms."

—C, preschool teacher

"I think, as an educator, what really matters to me is to support the children and their families. It would be so helpful as part of the education process to have had resources to identify and address the most supportive way to [communicate with] these families."

—C, preschool teacher

IN SUMMARY

You can use this checklist to help keep track of the suggestions made in this section:

☐ Check your own reactions to children, both verbal and nonverbal, for markers that indicate judgement or preference related to gender expression or roles.

☐ Consider how bias influences your interactions with children and families.

☐ Monitor your language and incorporate more gender-neutral language.

☐ Group children without using gender, and avoid separating children along gender lines.

☐ Set an expectation for respect in your classroom.

☐ Confront and correct gender stereotypes.

☐ Carefully review your classroom library for the following:

• Inclusion of books with gender-diverse themes and/or plots

• Inclusion of books with gender-diverse characters, nonheteronormative family structures, and books that upset gender stereotypes

• Removal of books that contain harmful or noninclusive gender messages

☐ Pay attention to how you read books to the children. Consider the questions you might ask and ways to engage children in conversation.

☐ Notice where children spend their time, and combine, rearrange, or add materials as needed to help offer new enticements and invitations to play.

☐ Diversify classroom materials, toys, and costumes, and pay attention to gendered use of color.

☐ Invite guest speakers or visitors who subvert gender stereotypes.

☐ Ensure that colors, jobs, toys, games, materials, and so on are not gendered in your classroom.

☐ Incorporate open-ended materials into learning areas.

☐ Celebrate all children and avoid tokenism.

GUIDANCE FOR SUPPORTING **GENDER DIVERSITY** IN EARLY CHILDHOOD EDUCATION

CHAPTER 5:

THE ROLE OF THE EARLY CHILDHOOD ADMINISTRATOR

Early childhood administrators work as a team with the ECE classroom teachers, aides, and support staff working in the classrooms of their program. You are encouraged to also read and utilize the strategies outlined in Chapter 4: The Role of the Early Childhood Teacher to supplement the information in this section.

TIPS FOR EARLY CHILDHOOD PROGRAMS

SETTING THE TONE

As an administrator, you help set the tone and create the culture of your center and program. Your support and advocacy can make a huge difference in how children, families, and your staff feel about your program. If you work with other administrators, meeting to discuss these ideas and concepts can help you have a unified approach as you work to support your staff in making possible changes to their practices and classrooms and can ensure that parents and families are met with consistent information and language.

> "On a personal level, I place so much value on the importance of establishing a community very early on in the school year. If the children don't see themselves as part of that community, or if they isolate themselves by gender, we just aren't a cohesive group. I believe that stereotypic gender roles often stifle the natural process of social and emotional growth in early childhood development."
>
> —C, preschool teacher

Using gender-neutral language (GNL) is one example of a change you can make as an administrator (see chapter 4). Reviewing your website, printed materials, and internal documents for potential edits to make language more gender inclusive is a great step in helping set a welcoming tone.

You can create a school or program culture of acceptance that can help support not just the children and families in your program but also your colleagues and staff. For example, sharing your own pronouns in introductions, in your email signature, or during meetings will show that you are aware of pronoun diversity and that you care about using the correct pronouns for the people you work with.

Consider the expectations you set (both explicitly and implicitly) for behavior—not just of the children in the program but of yourself and fellow staff as well. Explicit expectations are stated directly ("You need to submit your vacation request at least two weeks in advance."). Implicit expectations are conveyed by your actions or inaction. For example, ignoring a gender-stereotyped statement from a teacher during a staff meeting implies that you agree with their perspective or that it is acceptable within the program. When administrators set expectations, employees tend to meet those expectations, so make sure that your expectations are positive and affirming. A hostile school or work environment, including an environment that does not protect privacy or that misgenders individuals, violates anti-discrimination laws. It's okay for

GUIDANCE FOR SUPPORTING **GENDER DIVERSITY** IN EARLY CHILDHOOD EDUCATION

you to say, "I am learning more about this myself, but our program values all of our employees, children, and families. Let's work together to remember this."

Take a look at your marketing materials. In addition to reviewing materials such as flyers, business cards, posters, advertisements, and your website for GNL, you can use your marketing materials to show that your program values gender creativity. Images showing gender-creative children and a broad range of students can help identify your program as friendly without explicitly stating so in your materials. This can work well for programs that are corporately controlled. Perhaps you don't have the ability to make changes to the program mission statement (see below), but you could ensure that the images you share from your particular site are inclusive of gender diversity.

Staff and administration can and should work together to shift policy and culture. As an administrator, you may encounter staff who are reluctant or averse to considering gender diversity in the ways promoted in this book. You can let staff know that whether they agree or not, they need to uphold the values of the program: "You do not have to change your beliefs to work here, but you do have to treat all children and families with respect."

If you need further research to back up the benefits of creating more gender-neutral ECE spaces, consider Swedish preschools. Preschools in Sweden commonly use a gender-neutral pronoun, *hen*, to refer to individual children, address a group as *friends* rather than "boys and girls," and avoid gendered labels for toys and activities. A 2017 study conducted by Swedish and American psychologists found that children in such gender-neutral ECE spaces were "more willing to play with unfamiliar peers of the opposite sex and made fewer gender-stereotypical assumptions about them" (Joel and Vikhanski, 2019).

PROGRAM PHILOSOPHY AND MISSION STATEMENTS

One of the main ways that prospective families and employees start to narrow down programs and decide which is a good fit is by perusing each program's philosophy and mission statement. While corporately controlled programs do not have much independence in making changes to philosophy and mission statement (as these are typically uniform across the various franchise locations of the corporation), programs that are able to edit their statements can set a gender-justice tone that can advertise your program's commitment to gender inclusion from the outset. Many ECE program mission statements include language about valuing diversity—sometimes all it takes is adding the words "gender identity" to an existing list of diverse qualities.

Regardless of the style or length of your mission statement, it's important to consider the ways in which it expresses support and value for diversity and differences of all types. And, of course, once you have a mission statement, it's important to make sure that the practices of your program align with the values expressed in your mission and philosophy.

Prospective and new families are typically provided with parent handbooks and other materials. Review the explanations of your program's philosophy, and consider adding resources to help families understand the language your program will use around gender. Doing so can help you avoid problems and conflicts down the road, if families are aware that your program supports children in their gender exploration and identity development from the beginning. Families deserve to choose programs that are a good fit for them. And for families who are unaware of gender issues, sharing your program's philosophy publicly and matter-of-factly can provide a great opportunity for further learning and conversation.

REBECCA'S REFLECTION

Our daughter was almost six when she started kindergarten. She didn't qualify for any sort of pre-K the year prior, and she had never been in school before, so we decided to enroll her in a homeschool program when she was five-and-a-half. This gave her the opportunity to take a few classes before starting at our elementary school the following fall. We were so glad we had made that decision when school started that September. She'd already experienced being away from me, started learning to trust and take instruction from other adults, and make friendships not shaped by whoever her mom befriended. She transitioned into the classroom pretty easily and felt a strong sense of community with "her" class and "her" teacher and "her" friends.

On the other hand, our son's birthday is in June, meaning he would turn five shortly before kindergarten started. We worried about him being younger than most of his peers—especially because his social transition had not only been an emotional experience but also a time-consuming one. We wanted him to have space to just feel good in his own skin. When our daughter was home the first half of her fifth year, he had a playmate, but when she was in school, he was at loose ends. We figured enrolling him in preschool for one year would allow us to hold off on kindergarten until just after he turned six.

Finding support for our son and our family when he transitioned had been a struggle. Finding a preschool we could afford that would honor our son and help us navigate the new stuff (toileting anxiety, preferred name, preschool potty-humor discomfort) was impossible. Most places I called did not have any policies related to gender identity. They often said they'd have their director get back to me, but they never did. They all offered unhelpful, skeptical platitudes like, "There's never been anyone like that here, and I've been here twenty years," or "Oh, just enroll [him], get [him] around kids [his] age and it'll blow over," or "Does [he] need a special needs school, maybe?" We knew once our son was in public school, we would have more protection in requesting guidelines and support from the educators and administrators. But it had not occurred to me that my son would have to miss out on preschool to be safe. His best chance for a great start was another year at home or enrolling in kindergarten just after his fifth birthday.

He was so eager to go to school like his big sister that we went ahead and let him start kindergarten that fifth year. I don't know if that was the best choice, but it's the one we made and it went pretty poorly. Tantrums happened almost every single day on the way into class and on the way out. He struggled with the time away from me and the academics. It was very clear to us how much he would have benefited from more time to mature in a less-structured environment. It felt awful knowing we couldn't access a system I had assumed was for all children—one I had worked in for more than fifteen years. I realized then how important it is for ECE teachers to be educated in this area.

As a parent, it hurts when someone who works in child care denies your child their existence, their experience, and their needs. These things are the very foundation and central idea of early education. ECE teachers are often the first nonrelated faces that children look to for acceptance, comfort, and safety. They shape how our children feel about learning and their autonomy away from home and mold their first true friendships. Every child deserves that opportunity, vulnerable children especially. I think it's important to note, too, that the earlier children feel comfortable sharing their feelings and being confident in who they are, the less they struggle later. ECE teachers have such a powerful role and an amazing opportunity to encourage every child to feel good about themselves.

PROGRAM POLICIES

Internally, your program policies are a perfect place to outline practices that you want to represent your program values and priorities. The best thing that ECE programs can do is to discuss gender diversity and implement policies *before* they are a necessity, before a problem arises. While it can be tempting to think that you can avoid developing policies related to gender identity if you haven't yet had a child in your program who is transgender or overtly gender creative, it's actually better to consider ways you can make your program safe, welcoming, and respectful of all children before there is a "need."

Take a look at the policies for children and employees. You may want specific policies outlining your program's approach to supporting children's gender development and identity or prohibiting discrimination based on gender identity or expression. Your program's hiring policy may also need to be revised to explicitly protect applicants who are gender diverse in identity or expression. Additionally, review your school's dress codes to remove different expectations for dress based on gender. For example, instead of specifying genders—"Girls should not wear spaghetti-strap tops or wear shorts that are more than two inches above the knee"—change the language to "Children should not... ." If the dress code that requires particular attire for school performances or picture day that differ based on gender, alter the language to be more inclusive. (For more examples of gender-inclusive dress codes, see https://www.genderinclusiveschools.org/locker-rooms)

Luckily, there are several reputable and legitimate online resources to help schools in crafting policies relating to gender identity and diversity.

Gay, Lesbian, and Straight Education Network (GLSEN)

http://www.glsen.org

This is a national organization committed to supporting educators to support their students as well as raise up youth-led initiatives and programs. GLSEN conducts research, provides curricular resources and other support to teachers, and acts as an advocacy organization for policy and legislative change. Their website contains many resources for educators, including detailed examples of school policies.

Schools in Transition: A Guide for Supporting Transgender Students in K–12 Schools

https://www.aclu.org/sites/default/files/field_document/schools_in_transition_6.3.16.pdf

This sixty-eight-page guide produced by the American Civil Liberties Union, Gender Spectrum, the Human Rights Campaign Foundation, National Education Association, and National Center for Lesbian Rights provides guidance to assist school staff in supporting students. While it is focused on K–12 programs, many of the general concepts and policy suggestions are relevant for ECE programs as well.

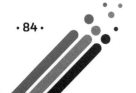

Welcoming Schools

http://www.welcomingschools.org/

An offshoot of the Human Rights Campaign, Welcoming Schools is one of the most abundant sources of relevant resources for teachers, administrators, and school programs looking for resources and support in improving their gender-affirming practices. Administrators are particularly encouraged to visit this site for specific policy-development resources.

FORMS AND PAPERWORK

If you aren't yet ready to create a specific policy related to gender identity or gender diversity, you can still make simple adjustments to paperwork to ensure inclusivity. Consider the forms that parents are asked to fill out, such as intake, history, wellness, and so on, as well as daily paperwork such as sign-in sheets and activity logs. Wherever possible, remove binary designations, such as *Mr.,* *Mrs.,* and *Ms.,* and provide blanks for people to fill out designations that fit for them. Don't just add an "other" category—this makes anything other than the binary responses seem odd or unusual. Instead of asking for the names and contact information of a child's *mother* and *father*, consider changing the language to "Parent/Guardian 1" and "Parent/Guardian 2." Not only does this remove binary gender assumptions, it is also less heteronormative, making your paperwork more inclusive for various types of families. Intake and family-history forms can ask for the child's preferred name, which might be different than what's on the child's birth certificate, and do not necessarily need to ask for the child's gender at all.

ECE programs may participate in funding grants or programs that necessitate collecting and reporting legal names, gender breakdowns per classroom, and so on. When this is required, reporting can be done to meet the criteria of the grant or funding source, but internal materials can use the children's preferred names and remove categorization of gender completely.

All paperwork in your program can incorporate gender-neutral or gender-inclusive language, and all school materials should reflect a child's chosen or preferred name. It is also important to keep details about a child's identity confidential. You may have children enrolled in the program who have transitioned socially and have birth certificates or legal documents that share the gender assigned at birth. That information does not need to be and should not be shared throughout your program to staff or families.

If parents complain about or oppose any of your program's policies around gender, focus on determining what their real concerns are rather than attempting to defend your policies. In chapter 6 we offer more guidance on communicating with families.

PROFESSIONAL DEVELOPMENT AND STAFF TRAININGS

Offering professional development and staff training related to gender diversity can serve as a productive method of building unity and buy-in for changing policies. These can be self-led, including gender-awareness assessments and classroom audits to help identify gaps in support (as mentioned in chapter 3), or externally led by organizations that offer specific gender-support training for school staff. Ideally, all teachers, administrators, substitutes, and support staff should participate in professional development and receive training related to gender diversity to ensure continuity of support and consistency of response. Numerous organizations offer professional development and school/teacher training on gender awareness. Some of the best include the following:

Welcoming Schools

https://www.welcomingschools.org/training/request-a-training/

In addition to offering in-person and remote training, the Welcoming Schools website contains a variety of resources for school administrators designed to help support gender diversity education. Welcoming Schools is a rich resource not to be missed!

Gender Spectrum

https://genderspectrum.org/articles/professional-development-educators

Gender Spectrum offers training programs ranging from one-time to yearlong programs for school staff. The website has additional resources as well. A well-regarded resource for all educators.

TransFamily Support Services

https://www.transfamilysos.org/services/training-education/

TransFamily Support Services, which is local to San Diego County, California, has a strong reputation of working with San Diego–area school districts, programs, and professionals, offering training around gender education, diversity, trans issues, and sensitivity. Virtual trainings are also available.

If you are interested in self-led trainings and reflective assessments and audits, *Supporting Gender Diversity in Early Childhood Classrooms: A Practical*

Guide (2019) by Encian Pastel et al. is a strong resource for early childhood educators and contains numerous assessment and audit tools to assist the ECE program in developing gender-supportive practices. It is written by the team behind Gender Justice in Early Childhood Education (https://www.genderjusticeinearlychildhood.com/). Many of the tools are available on the website as well.

Your program might also consider offering gender-education events and resources for children and families. An event could be as elaborate as a family-education evening led by external trainers or as simple as information and resources shared via the parent bulletin boards and classroom newsletters. Families who are initially skeptical or resistant to some of your gender-neutral or gender-supportive practices may be won over when they see what gender education really looks like in the classroom and how their own child benefits from a more gender-expansive environment.

When providing training at your school, resist the temptation to use individual children or families in your program as examples or illustrative training tools. Although a particular child may be the impetus for you to offer gender-based professional development to your staff, the child and family deserve privacy. It's not appropriate to disclose personal information about any child or family at your program (past or present) to improve or personalize training.

ADVOCACY FOR INCLUSION

In general, you can include gender diversity in any of your existing diversity initiatives. In addition to marketing materials, website images, and so on, consider how you could include gender diversity in your building decor. Think about your signage for parent spaces and staff rooms. Is there anything present that is cis- or heteronormative or upholds the gender binary? You can also involve your stakeholders. If you have any sort of parent organization, they may be great allies in helping develop your gender-diversity policies. If you undertake collaborative efforts with community members, agencies, or other centers, consider how you might be able to advocate for gender-diversity education. Your actions at your site may help spread awareness and bring about change in the wider community!

THE BATHROOM DEBATE

One of the biggest controversies surrounding transgender people in the United States is the use of public restrooms. The purported concern over people using the bathroom that is appropriate for their gender identity is that it would provide opportunity and protection for sexual predators and is often used as a screen to gain support for anti-trans legislation and policies. There is **no** increased risk of assault or predation due to bathroom access, even in mixed-gender bathrooms. In states with longstanding laws allowing people to use bathrooms aligned with their gender identity, there is no increased reported criminal activity (Steinmetz, 2016). Activists and politicians who discriminate against people who are gender diverse have had success in preying upon people's worst fears about transgender people. The bathroom debate has been the subject of myriad articles, op-eds, documentaries, protests, school-board fights, and litigation all the way to the Supreme Court of the United States.

For older children and adults, the least disruptive scenario is allowing the use of the bathroom most closely matching the person's gender identity. For example, a transwoman who is forced to use a men's restroom or a transman who is forced to use a women's restroom could cause more ruckus and fear than if they used the restroom that aligned with their gender expression. Ideally, gender-neutral or single-user restrooms would be available in all places that currently have gendered restrooms. Many businesses, restaurants, schools, and offices have had great success with making all previously gender-segregated bathrooms gender neutral. After all, most people use gender-neutral bathrooms every day—the bathrooms in private homes are seldom gender segregated!

K–12 schools have various choices and decisions to make about their policies for bathroom use. In these settings, groups of children are often using the restroom together, frequently without adult supervision. To avoid parental concerns or controversy, many schools choose to allow gender-diverse

students to use a separate bathroom, often one that is in the administrative area. However, this avoidance makes things unequal and difficult for children and is not a model of access and inclusion. Schools that have followed recommended practice and allowed children to use the bathroom that fits best with their gender expression or identity have typically seen no problems or issues, but this remains one of the biggest areas of concern that administrators for K–12 schools have about supporting gender-diverse students.

In the ECE setting, the concerns are different. Early childhood environments seldom offer gender-separated bathrooms for the children's use. For example, in California, Community Care Licensing requires visual supervision of all children by an adult at all times, including in the bathroom, so many classrooms have open bathroom spaces in their classrooms. There are sometimes dividers between toilets, but there are seldom stalls in an ECE setting. ECE care providers who work with infants, toddlers, and young children with delayed toilet training are changing diapers throughout the day. All of this creates a situation in which it is nearly impossible for a child who might be trans or who is living as a gender that does not "match" with their genitals to avoid disclosure to their teachers and sometimes their classmates.

The general advice for best practice for working with gender-diverse children is to recognize that there is no need to ask or know about children's bodies. But what if you are responsible for changing diapers? The best thing to do is to recognize that all children deserve bodily autonomy and privacy. You may have a young child in your program who has transitioned socially. Allow that child to use the bathroom that fits best for them, and recognize that some children or families may request that their child have more privacy when using the restroom. Because young children are often using the restroom next to one another without visual barriers, there may be natural curiosity ("Why is he sitting down to pee?"). In our experience this curiosity is present in all children, regardless of gender identity. Remember to just answer the question the child is asking; there is no need to go into detail or offer more information than is being asked for or to compromise a child's autonomy and privacy. Be matter-of-fact in your response: "That is how he feels most comfortable." There is no one-size-fits-all approach, but as an administrator, it's important to recognize that you may need to help teachers feel supported to support their students.

CONSISTENCY OF CULTURE

You get to create the culture of your program. What messages do you want to send to current and prospective families and the community about your program? As an administrator, you have the responsibility to ensure consistency in your program and support adherence to school policies and philosophy. Doing so may involve working more specifically on particular areas of your program or spending more time assisting individual teachers and staff. If you commit to developing and maintaining a partnership with all of your staff that involves learning from mistakes, self-reflection, program audits, and a desire to seek more and new information, you will be creating a program that is a safe, welcoming, and respectful space for *all* children and families.

"The **only** negative experience at her nursery school (where she attended from eighteen months until age three) was when she potty trained at age two and started coming in with "girl" underwear (she was still mostly in "boy" clothes then). Her teacher told her, 'You tell your mom not to buy you these girl underwear. They don't fit your parts!' (For what it's worth, they absolutely fit around her body just fine.) [Our child] cried at pickup, telling me, 'L says I can't wear my Dory underwear because they're for girls and my penis won't fit.' I have a close relationship with this teacher, so needless to say, I marched right back in there and let her have a piece of my mind (as politely as I could). That was the end of that. From then on while she attended that school, anything E wore, said, or did that was gender nonconforming was embraced and accepted and no problem."

—C, mother of a 7-year-old transgender daughter and a 9-year-old cisgender son

EDUCATOR PERSPECTIVES:
WHAT ECE PROFESSIONALS
WANT FROM THEIR
ADMINISTRATORS

"I would like our administration to provide (mandatory) training and education for educators and staff (and parent education). I don't feel there is clear or consistent messaging from our organization."

—A, early elementary teacher

"[I would like] more proactive strategies. I feel we are very supportive when we see it but [are] not necessarily proactive."

—J, toddler teacher

"Our fears of sending our daughter to preschool were all surrounding gender identity. After the first few weeks, we laughed as our concerns had shifted to more "typical" preschool concerns such as tears at drop off. Over time, more issues surrounding gender identity did arise at school, but for a moment it was nice to feel like our worries were more typical of other parents of preschoolers."

—D, father to a 4-year-old transgender daughter and a 2-year-old child

"I would want the school to teach kiddos about gender and how they might experience it. I remember school as a kid being about reinforcing gender assignment more than actually understanding gender."

—B, trans father to a toddler

"[I would like] a more overt stance that supports social justice, diversity, and inclusion, opportunities to regularly assess and critique aspects of the program to be more inclusive, and more professional development/learning for staff."

—S, early elementary teacher

"I would love to have had my own administration already have an educated response and protocol to gender expression, one that supports the family and the child and negates the stereotypes that are rooted in the ECE system."

—C, preschool teacher

IN SUMMARY

You can use this checklist to help keep track of the suggestions made in this section.

☐ Review program website, printed materials, and internal documents for gender-neutral language.

☐ Share your own pronouns in introductions, your email signature, and/or during meetings.

☐ Review marketing materials for inclusive imagery of gender-creative children.

☐ Make edits to your program philosophy and mission statements to reflect gender inclusivity.

☐ Ask yourself if the practices of your program align with your mission and philosophy.

☐ Edit, revise, or create school policies, including:

• Supporting children's gender development and identity

• Prohibiting discrimination based on gender identity or expression

• Hiring policies protecting applicants who are gender diverse

• Dress codes

☐ Edit and revise forms and paperwork, including:

- Removing binary designations (*Mr./Mrs./Ms.*) and replacing with a blank, if needed

- Replacing *Mother* and *Father* with "Parent/Guardian 1" and "Parent/Guardian 2"

- Asking for chosen name (vs. legal name) and using it on all school materials

- Removing questions asking for reporting of a child's gender

- Completing self-assessments and classroom/program audits to determine areas where gender support is needed

- Considering methods of offering professional development focused on gender diversity, to staff and families in your program

- Collaborating with parent organizations, community members and agencies, and other centers for joint gender-diversity education efforts

- Reviewing your signage for restrooms, staff rooms, and so on. Are there any changes to be made to make your spaces more inclusive?

CHAPTER 6:

SUPPORT FOR FAMILIES: ENSURING POSITIVE COMMUNICATION ABOUT GENDER DIVERSITY

Early childhood educators know that communication with families is one of their primary tasks that helps build relationships and create positive home-school connections. Most early childhood educators have more regular communication (often daily) with their students' families than the teachers of elementary or older children do. While much of this communication revolves around caregiving routines and daily updates about a child's progress and experiences, early childhood educators commonly communicate with families about concerns, challenges, successes, and resources for support.

There is a variety of potential conversations you may need or want to have with families about gender diversity. Consider the following topics:

- You are making changes to your program to increase gender diversity and want to inform families.

- You are meeting with a parent to discuss their child's development and experience in your classroom (parent/teacher conferences).

- You want to learn more from a family about how best to support their gender-diverse child.

Each of these scenarios would necessitate a different conversation, but all of them would require empathetic, active listening combined with confidence and support. Following are some general tips and strategies to increase the effectiveness of your conversations with families on the subject of gender.

WHERE FAMILIES ARE COMING FROM

Families approach the topic of gender diversity just as any of us do—from a place that is informed by their experiences, education, culture, religion, values, beliefs, and biases. A parent or guardian may be the one who brings their child's gender diversity to your attention, or you may be the person helping provide insight to a family member about behavior or development you are seeing in the classroom. If you are talking to all the families in your classroom about classroom practices, curriculum, or policies related to gender diversity, you may be communicating to people who are brand-new to this topic.

For children who are gender diverse, parental reactions can vary. Some parents are on board with affirmative support from the beginning; others question whether a young child can really "know" their own gender. There is often a desire on the part of adults to make sure children "know for sure" before the family takes any action to affirm the child's gender. This is, unfortunately, impossible because we can never be 100 percent certain of another person's identity. It is worth noting that nobody asks cisgender children if they are absolutely sure about their gender before treating the child accordingly.

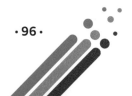

Having a child who is transgender or gender diverse is difficult in some way for nearly all parents, even for those with lots of knowledge and experience. Parents often recognize the realities of the potential difficulties for their child and may also have to manage their own changing expectations and plans. Even with increased societal awareness and access to information, gender diversity in young children can still be challenging for adults.

REBECCA'S REFLECTION

Since our children were born, I have been the primary parent—the one who does the pickups and drop-offs, the one who handles colds and fevers, bad dreams, and dentist appointments. I have learned to tune in to my kids, their specific rhythms and anxieties. Your very survival as a parent depends on your ability to weed out the whining from the needs, and you learn quickly what is desire and what is desperation. When our son first announced to us that he was a boy, we told him he was mistaken. Over time, based on recommendations from experts to watch for him to be insistent, consistent, and persistent, we told him we heard him and we slowly integrated changes to allow him to transition socially (for us this included an affirming hairstyle, clothing, pronouns, and name). This guidance is consistent with current best practice, which means that most kids who identify as transgender or nonbinary have been extraordinarily patient. Their needs are emergent, and they are rarely equipped to offer insight or education.

Most times when we talk about challenges kids face, it's from a perspective that their childhood experiences are relatively relatable. Being transgender or nonbinary or even just exploring and pushing back on gender norms is still a very charged topic. It's paramount that, when kids struggle with this, their caretakers are informed and educated on the topic to help the family and to best support the child. Often when we discuss gender-expansiveness awareness in education, we start from an assumption that the family has already accepted the child. Parents look to educators to help them navigate unexpected challenges and experiences. The more educators understand the nuances of gender, the more capable they are of guiding families. Every child who is gender expansive is not trans or nonbinary; in fact, they rarely are. But every child who is gender expansive deserves an opportunity to explore what that means for them. Avoiding gender norms in your language and activities and allowing children to ask questions and assert themselves should be standard in any classroom.

Parents or family members may come to you as strong advocates for their child who already have lots of education and knowledge, or they may come to you with lots of questions. Regardless, our job as their child's ECE provider is to offer support backed up by evidence-based best practices.

FRAMING THE CONVERSATION

It's important to make conversations about gender developmentally appropriate. Place emphasis on the ways in which making your classroom more gender diverse benefits all of the children. Again, you set the tone and philosophy for your classroom culture. "Normalizing gender as a spectrum is one of the best ways to create a safe environment for families and to teach inclusion" (McCulloch, 2019).

If you are sharing information with families about the ways your program is going to be increasing its gender diversity, focus on bringing the parents along with you on the learning journey. This will help reduce pushback from parents who are uncomfortable with gender conversations. Remember, talking about gender is **not** talking about sex. Helping parents understand the differences between gender and sex and sexual orientation can help eliminate statements such as, "I don't want you talking about sex with my child," or "Stop sexualizing children." Stay away from LGBTQ+ or other acronyms when discussing gender with adults about young children; the acronyms lump sexual orientation in with gender and can frame the conversation in a way that makes hesitant adults uncomfortable. Additionally, conversation should never be about sexual orientation or genitals when discussing children's gender.

As you become more comfortable with gender diversity and become familiar with creating a gender-expansive classroom, you'll find yourself changing the way you speak about gender. For example, during conferences and updates, you might avoid categorizing children's playmates based on gender, such as "Dylan plays mainly with the girls." Instead, focus on the types of play and the quality of peer relationships. Putting emphasis on gender in these ways implies that there are acceptable—and less acceptable—playmates for children based on their gender.

You may worry about how to respond to parents who are not supportive of gender expansiveness in your program. The Virtual Lab School online training program "Creating Gender Safe Spaces" (see appendix A) offers a great deal of information and training around how to appropriately respond to difficult statements or conflict, such as the following suggestions:

- If family members express anger or disapproval about the inclusion of books, pictures, or materials that reflect gender-diverse families, you

could say, "We want to make sure that all children in our program see their families represented so they feel valued. We have lots of books that show a mom and a dad, also (Virtual Lab School, n.d.)."

- If family members are upset by the program's commitment to allow transgender children to participate in the program in a way that matches their identity, you could say, "We work to make sure that every child is safe and respected in the program (Virtual Lab School, n.d.)."

- If someone makes negative comments about children or their families, you can state: "My job is to help ensure the safety and security of all the children in our program. It is not a choice to say those comments here (Virtual Lab School, n.d.)."

- If a family member is upset, angry, or disapproving of your program's support for gender expansiveness, inform your program manager or training and curriculum specialist so they can provide additional support (Virtual Lab School, n.d.).

Another great resource to help educators respond to concerns about being gender inclusive is the handout *Be Prepared for LGBTQ Questions and Concerns* (Human Rights Campaign Foundation and Welcoming Schools, 2019), which offers guidance, research, and strategies for responding to parents and coworkers. See appendix A for a link to this resource.

Additional strategies for responding to questions and concerns about a child's gender expression are outlined in *Healthy Gender Development and Young Children: A Guide for Early Childhood Programs and Professionals* (National Center on Parent, Family, and Community Engagement, n.d.). See appendix A for a link to this report.

When you are talking with a parent who is feeling discomfort or upset about their child's gender expression or identity, it can be tempting for administrators and teachers to minimize behavior in an attempt to alleviate familial discomfort. Try to avoid saying things such as, "She's just a tomboy," or "He'll grow out of it," and instead help families accept each child where they are at that time. It's important that we trust children when they say, "This is who I am" (Virtual Lab School, n.d.). We can be strong advocates for the child and help families feel more comfortable with who their child may be.

> "Sometimes the parents of the child who was gender expansive would make comments that they didn't like their son dressing up or playing with dolls. I would typically make a comment to the parent, noting what I saw in the moment ('Your son is caring so well for that baby doll. He must see how you are with his

baby sister.'). Our classroom staff is very accepting in that all the materials are available for anyone who wants to explore."

—C, toddler teacher

Making the effort to frame gender conversations as normal, expected, and a method of ensuring optimal development and inclusion for all children will go a long way in helping you have productive interactions with the families you work with.

PARENTS AS EXPERTS

Parents are the experts on their own child. Families are valuable resources and can help you as the ECE professional understand their child most fully. However, it is common for teachers and administrators to rely heavily on the parents of gender-diverse children to provide education and training for teachers and staff. It's important to remember that parents are looking for help, too; they don't want to always have to train or teach others how to appropriately interact with their child. Parents should not have to be teachers for their child's teacher. On the other hand, some parents will welcome or request the opportunity to provide information or training to program staff to help make the program a safer place for their child. In some instances, this can be beneficial; many parents have a wealth of knowledge. But before you rely on parents to provide training, consider ways you can seek training on behalf of the program without putting the burden of education on the families. Taking steps toward learning more and doing research will help build trust between you and the families and show that you are being proactive in providing the best possible program for their child.

Please try not to ask parents, "What should we do?" Nearly all parents with a gender-diverse child appreciate programs where the teachers and administrators take a proactive role in developing policies and practices to protect and support their child if those policies are not already in place. While parents should be asked about their child and how best to support them, parents of gender-diverse children should not be asked those questions at a more intensive level than any other parent would be asked.

Additionally, it is common for parents of gender-diverse children to be asked intrusive questions about their child's genitalia and medical history. While it's never appropriate for K–12 teachers to ask parents or children questions about a child's genitalia, ECE teachers are often helping children with diapering or toileting. Instead of asking about genitalia (unless you are asking the question

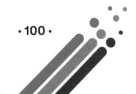

of all parents about their children), it is possible for you to go with the flow rather than asking pointed personal questions.

When you encounter families who disclose to you that their child is transgender, it is important that you recognize that, for the vast majority of families, this disclosure and acceptance came after months or years of soul-searching, research, and discovery. It takes courage and vulnerability for a parent to disclose their child's transgender status to a teacher, and it can be very hurtful to have their journey invalidated by being asked, "Are you sure?" or being told their child is just confused or that they are doing the wrong thing. It is not your role to second-guess or deny. *Raising the Transgender Child* by Michele Angello and Ali Bowman (2016) offers many strategies and tips for helping meet families where they are when they disclose.

REBECCA'S REFLECTION

As a parent, there comes a point in your child's transition experience at which you have to let a large number of people know what's going on gender-wise and what moving forward looks like. Some parents announce their child's transition on social media or email their relatives and close friends. Others might make phone calls prior to the next (and new first) time that someone will be seeing their child. For the parents, and especially for the child, it is an exhaustive amount of emotional labor. In early childhood, honoring a child's identity is primarily a matter of language—there is no medical intervention or support. The expectation of other adults is only to use the appropriate pronouns and names, just language. Not everyone reacts supportively. By the time most parents disclose their child's gender identity to their child's teacher, they have already been questioned, threatened, denied, accused and, often, cast out of at least one if not more community support systems (extended family, church, team sport, etc.). It's so important to remember your role as an educator is to support each child, no matter what they are experiencing and no matter how they show up.

We have been lucky to have a number of incredible educators in our children's lives. They have all been supportive of my son and happy to include gender-expansive books in their class libraries. But the most powerful connections have been with teachers who see his experience and want to improve it by having whole-class conversations about gender and fashion and hair length, by being supportive of gender expression and exploration in general. When I asked my son how it feels when the teacher talks about stuff like that in group time or circle time, he said, "It's nice because it's like she cares about people who are transgender or, like, want to wear skirts or are nonbinary or have long hair, like she knows about them and it's okay. Like, she's not just doing it to be nice to me because I'm in her actual class." I found this to be incredibly powerful because it means kids, young kids, can clearly see who recognizes their struggle and supports them, versus who is tolerating their experience. True understanding can take time and education, but being able to see the child's exploration or identity as valid should be there from the very start.

We must recognize that parents are experts on their child within the context of their experience. As ECE professionals, we can also offer knowledge and information that can be helpful. Parents are also not necessarily spokespeople for entire communities. Recognize and respect the individuality of the families you work with.

> "A collaborative relationship between parents/families and educators can have such a positive impact on students. Some of my greatest learning moments as a teacher have come from parents feeling comfortable sharing their knowledge or concerns with me. We all come from our own experiences and biases, so this additional insight from parents can be extremely valuable to expanding our perspective. While this collaborative relationship between parents and teachers is crucial, I think the onus of the work toward more equitable and supportive school environments should be on the educators. I believe the most powerful way we can support students is for the school administration to implement policies and practices that protect and affirm all student identities. All staff should have continual education and teaching resources to best support students. Creating a community built on trust and support shouldn't just be limited to some classrooms. It should be throughout the entire school, from when you walk in the doors to each classroom you enter. [Most school administrators] do not [teach] students [themselves] and are often disconnected from the real needs of students and families. Teachers can bridge this gap. They should be advocates for their students and families."
>
> —K, early elementary teacher

OPTIMIZING INTERACTIONS AND COMMUNICATION

The characteristics of active listening and empathetic dialogue that are commonly taught to educators to assist them in communicating with parents are, of course, relevant in these situations. However, there are some specific strategies that can increase the effectiveness of gender-based communications with families.

- Validate distress: "I know this is hard/awkward." "Yes, I can understand why that scares you." "Thank you for sharing your experience."

- Remind parents why gender diversity is important: "This is so helpful for our students."

- Acknowledge mistakes: If you make an error when communicating with a parent, for example, using the wrong pronoun, acknowledge your mistake, apologize, and move on.

- Offer reassurance: Assure family members that what you are doing in the classroom is worthy and that what they are doing is important.

- Acknowledge the learning curve: It's okay to admit what you don't know and show that you are open to learning.

- Help parents with their own discomfort: Provide a framework for helping parents work through their own discomfort: "You may hear values expressed that differ from your own."

- Point out common ground, especially when there is conflict: "We share a desire to help children express themselves authentically." It is crucial to validate parental reactions, even if those reactions are challenging. Doing so will help keep the lines of communication open between you and the parent.

- Acknowledge and affirm parental feelings: Stay true to good practice as you acknowledge the range of parental feelings. "We call all the children by their preferred names." "We see lots of gender exploration in all children; this is very normal."

- Use the Sandwich Method: When discussing concerns or pointing out issues to parents, sandwich the concern between two compliments and positives about the child/program/family.

BUILDING BRIDGES

Parents often admit they are afraid or don't know how to respond to something, but teachers and administrators seldom admit their own fears or lack of knowledge. Often ECE professionals feel as though they need to be seen as knowledgeable about everything related to children. It's okay to show your own vulnerability to parents: "This is an area where I need to learn more. I'll be doing some research right away." Try not to label parents as unsupportive; there are usually many layers of experience, fear, and so on that will affect how parents react the way they do. Try to treat the parents as your

PARENT PERSPECTIVES:
WHAT PARENTS WANT YOU TO KNOW ABOUT COMMUNICATION

"[When he was in preschool] we appreciated so much that the school stayed fluid and open."

—J, mother of a 13-year-old transgender son

"I wish that instead of teaching others, others could have taught me. The more families that are willing to come forward make it easier for everyone. We didn't want to be the poster child for this or be in the media, but we had to speak out to make sure there was a resource for other families."

—H, mother of a 14-year-old transgender son and a 12-year-old cisgender daughter

"I wish that my pediatrician [had] had enough gender education to start a conversation with me when he first saw my kid walk into his office dressed in girly tops. I feel that if the conversation had started earlier, I would have understood and supported earlier. I wish that I had found the gender-specific conferences earlier, as they were an amazing way to learn so much. I used peer-support groups, conferences, and individual therapy for myself to increase my knowledge and ability to support my kid."

—C, mother of a 14-year-old transgender daughter and an 11-year-old cisgender son

allies. Parents who are reluctant will often respond well to being partners in the journey with you.

Remember that serving one child or family or person well has a ripple effect. You have the power of being a responsive ally for a family—and the possibility of being a positive memory when they tell the story of their child's early years. You have the potential to set the stage for change within your classroom. The way you approach gender diversity in your classroom could have wide-reaching effects for the children and families you work with.

> "It's been hard to connect with other parents/families going through what we were with our kid, so we often felt really isolated. If it weren't for the internet, we would have been so lost, but even virtual connections have been hard to find. We also really struggled to find a therapist in our area who could work with both adults and children, who specialized in gender-nonconforming/trans kids situations. There's just no road map for socially transitioning the gender of one's young child, and it feels really scary and lonely, even when you are confident in your child's identity and that you're doing the right thing."
>
> **—C, mother of a 7-year-old trans-gender daughter and a 9-year-old cisgender son**

> "What I wish is that there was more support for nonbinary kids and parents. When [my son] shifted to being trans, there was so much more understanding that he got from the support systems and families who participate in them. There is a lot of pressure to fit into *boy* or *girl* and to 'fully' transition into one of them. What about all the kids that are happily a blend of both? Those kids need more support in our world."
>
> **—S, mother of a 9-year-old transgender son and two cisgender children**

> "Teachers need to communicate with parents. Parents don't always have all the information."
>
> **—K, mother of a 20-year-old transgender son and an adult cisgender daughter**

SHARING RESOURCES

The ECE program can be an important connection and resource for families. Information about gender diversity is valuable for *all* of the families in your program, not just families with children who are gender expansive. Consider putting books for both adults and children in your family lending library. In your newsletters and parent communications, treat gender diversity as normal in your classroom, and include examples when you share stories about the curriculum or what the children have been doing. Think about the photos you choose to share on your classroom sites or in parent communications— images can be powerful communicators of values and philosophy. Include photos of children of all genders engaged in the play they authentically enjoy. This does not always require commentary; simply presenting examples of how all the children in your class are able to exist and show up in your classroom is powerful.

There are many examples of resources in appendix A, including websites that are specifically helpful for families. Don't be afraid to seek information to pass on to parents who may be overwhelmed or not have easy access to information. You can be an important resource yourself just by sharing resources!

When considering taking steps to make their classroom or program more gender expansive, most teachers are afraid of negative reactions from parents, not from the children. It is important to remember that just like any curricular or philosophical choice you make for your program, choosing to make your classroom or program more welcoming and diverse is a choice you are allowed to make. *You* set the tone for your classroom or program. Additionally, you may be surprised at how little of a "splash" the changes outlined in the previous chapters actually make. A lot will depend on your parent community and the populations you serve. Many of the adjustments that will make your program more gender diverse are quite simple, such as changing the way you choose to group children for activities, while others, such as introducing discussion of gender diversity or pronouns, may require more conversation with families to ensure that everyone is informed and on board.

IN SUMMARY

Early childhood educators know that collaboration and communication with families help improve outcomes for children in their program. This approach is especially valuable when communicating with families about gender issues. Recognize that everyone is on a learning journey related to gender, and meet families where they are. Early childhood educators can respect families as experts on their own children while also serving as resources to the families for further learning and growth. Collaboration and communication lead to compassion!

CHAPTER 7:
IN THE FUTURE...

Gender diversity is just one piece in the puzzle of making your classroom and program an inclusive, welcoming place. Happily, taking even small steps will help move you toward your goal. Consider each minor change you might make in your practices to be a step toward ensuring that all of your children and families feel welcomed, seen, heard, and respected!

CONTINUING THE JOURNEY TOWARD INCLUSION

While the culture and climate in the United States today is generally more accepting of gender diversity than in the past, there is still much work to do. People who are gender diverse or transgender or identify in the LGBTQ+ spectrum face discrimination, bias, and very real threats of harm on a daily basis. This includes children and families. Much of the progress made during the Obama administration in terms of legal protection of rights and civil liberties for LGBTQ+ people was rolled back or eliminated under the Trump administration. As of this printing, the Biden administration has worked to extend protections, for example, by including transgender students in Title IX protections. Unfortunately, the political climate and division in the United States in recent years has contributed to backlash against progress. At the time of this writing in early 2022, individual states are actively working to pass extreme legislation criminalizing gender-affirmative care, prohibiting transgender children from using the appropriate bathroom, and preventing transgender or nonbinary children from participating in school and activities in alignment with their gender identity. Departments of education have issued directives that prohibit teachers from using a student's chosen name or pronouns, or in some cases, from even asking students what pronouns they use. Some school boards have disciplined teachers for displaying pride flags in their classrooms. In just one week in March 2022, Alabama, Alaska, Arizona, Florida, Idaho, Iowa, Indiana, Kentucky, Louisiana, Missouri, and Tennessee all advanced legislation directly attacking the safety and rights of transgender and gender diverse children and their parents. The sense of optimism and hope that was very real nearly a decade ago has diminished in recent years.

REBECCA'S REFLECTION

Shortly after we finished the first draft of this manuscript in late 2021, dozens of transphobic bills relating to the care and education of gender-diverse children went into legislation. Most of them mandate that discussing, labeling, acknowledging, or condoning, even passively, any child in regard to their gender or sexuality would be punishable by a court of law for both the parent and educator. While these issues are ongoing, I frequently get asked how I can even stand to read the news. In many ways, I can stand to read it because I am incredibly privileged. My son is light skinned. We live in Southern California. We have financial stability. I have a minimal and flexible work schedule that has enabled me to be at home with my children. My husband is a hands-on father. I am a healthy, white, cisgender woman whose family has an incredible support system. Take away any one of those things and my privilege is diminished and the impact of this legislation would be much more terrifying.

When my son transitioned, I had many conversations, often awkward at the outset, with incredible parents and their children. It's important to note that my son's peer group incorporates a wide variety of kids. He has friends who moved here from other states and countries, friends who have different religious beliefs from the traditions my son has grown up with, and friends who have parents who felt blindsided by the news. These conversations have been an honor and a humbling and overwhelmingly positive experience. Their willingness to know more and the opportunity to ask questions have been the primary reasons these conversations have gone so well. When I share with others that some people are born in a body or a pronoun that feels incompatible with their existence, children's responses are largely sympathetic, express similar personal feelings, and always, always, question what happens next. Who helps them? Because our family lives in California and are protected by our state's laws, I have always had an answer for this question.

There is a part of me that wants to jokingly note that none of the young children I have talked about gender with have transitioned during the writing of this book. While I recognize this may be an important statistic for the reader, it is wildly unimportant. What it shows, and what I think is so much more compelling, is that children are able to talk about gender and gender identity in developmentally appropriate ways, provided that the educator is sufficiently trained in the science and psychology of those two things, supported by their administration, and supplied with materials that reflect diversity. Lastly, it is important to note that to deny a child the opportunity to talk about things regarding their general sense of autonomy will affect the ability for parents and administrators to monitor the safety of that minor child in ways not related to gender or gender identity. If children are not free to talk because administrators and parents are not free to hear them, we lose the opportunity to help millions of children in thousands of ways.

Despite the current political landscape, we are seeing increased societal awareness, growing understanding and acceptance, and hope that rights and conditions will improve for the LGBTQ+ and gender-expansive community. Media depictions of those who are transgender and gender diverse continue to improve and be more widespread. Cultural shifts are occurring, and with those shifts, public perception and awareness grows.

FOR MORE INFORMATION

Lambda Legal

https://www.lambdalegal.org/know-your-rights#lgbtq-teens-amp-young-adults

This website has extensive information for teens and young adults related to their legal protections as LGBTQ+ youth. Sections with resources and information include bullying, speech, schools, and more.

Transgender Law Center

https://transgenderlawcenter.org/

National organization working to change legislation and policy for those who are transgender, including children. Website additionally provides information about various advocacy and support opportunities, as well as case summaries of relevant and noteworthy legal cases.

National Center for Transgender Equality

https://transequality.org/

Clearinghouse for advocacy and issues related to transgender rights. Specific issues such as aging, disability, voting rights, and more are highlighted, as well as calls for action. Legal advice related to educational rights for children who are transgender are also included. A wealth of resources and up-to-date information.

Transgender Students and School Bathrooms: Frequently Asked Questions

https://www.genderspectrum.org/articles/bathroom-faq

This publication illustrates the rights of students and the issues that arise for students and schools related to bathroom use. Endorsed by multiple

professional organizations, including the National Association of School Psychologists, this report offers guidance for school officials and provides a wealth of information.

Welcoming Schools Supportive Laws and Policies

https://www.welcomingschools.org/resources/research/supporting-laws-policies/

Provides overviews, downloads, and FAQs related to legislation and policies that help protect and support LGBTQ+ students.

TO-DO LIST

As ECE professionals, professional development is key to maintaining quality practices. To be the best teacher possible, it is necessary to continue learning and implementing new practices. If supporting gender diversity is important to you, here are a few items to add to your to-do list... and you might find that many of these are already in your practice!

- Recognize that there is **always** more to learn.

- Be open to changing your opinions when you learn new information.

- Understand that your experiences are not the experiences of the colleagues, children, and families you work with. Your world is not *the* world.

- Embrace a vision of inclusion for your program.

- Realize that information is constantly evolving—being a supportive ECE professional necessitates change.

- Value a growth mindset.

- Seek out new information and utilize the resources you have access to.

- Accept mistakes as learning opportunities—nobody is perfect!

- Actively call out bias and stereotypes.

- Welcome opportunities for authentic conversation about gender with children and families.

MAKING MISTAKES

It is inevitable that mistakes will be made. The language or terminology that is preferred by one person is disliked or found offensive by another. Concepts and ideas that are cutting edge one day are outdated the next. We have undoubtedly misspoken or made mistakes that unintentionally offend in this book, and we welcome the opportunity to learn more and do better as understanding evolves. We're all doing the best we can... most of the time. Everyone's an expert... on their own experience. Be curious, call people in, not out, and create a space where it's okay for everyone to learn from their mistakes.

IN CONCLUSION

The bottom line is this: children thrive when they are respected, protected, and given opportunities to explore the world and who they are. Opening our worldview to encompass the wide and vast diversity of the gender spectrum will only benefit us and the children we work with. Thank you for being open to considering ways you can make your ECE program more gender diverse. The world will be better for it!

For updates on legislation and policies related to education and gender diversity, see this book's page at https://www.gryphonhouse.com

APPENDICES

APPENDIX A:
RESOURCES FOR ECE PROFESSIONALS

The following is a curated list of relevant and potentially helpful resources that you can use in your classroom, with parents, or for professional development. This is not an exhaustive list; there are hundreds of resources available, both free and for a fee.

TRAININGS

Virtual Lab School, "Creating Gender Safe Spaces"

https://www.virtuallabschool.org/

Virtual Lab School offers free online professional development courses for ECE professionals. This course provides an overview of gender identity and development and offers resources, strategies, and lesson plans for ECE programs and providers. Videos, parent perspectives, and classroom examples are included, helping ECE programs provide optimal environments for gender-creative children. Highly recommended for all ECE professionals.

CLASSROOM RESOURCES

Pride and Less Prejudice

https://www.prideandlessprejudice.org/

Provides free LGBTQ+ themed books to preschool through third-grade classrooms to encourage inclusion, acceptance, visibility, and representation

Project Gender Balance

https://www.projectgenderbalance.com/

Offers pronoun stickers for children's books to help increase the amount of book equity in the classroom or home. Allows parents or teachers to change the gender and pronouns of picture-book characters

Everybody Can Like

http://elisegravel.com/en/blog/everybody-can-like/

This free, printable poster from artist Elise Gravel shows children that there is no such thing as "girl stuff" and "boy stuff."

Early Childhood Gender 101 Info Sheet

https://static1.squarespace.com/static/59689d4b3a0411170f5f65ce/t/61898f6 34be0d66d732733e8/1636405092063/Infosheet-v3.pdf

This well-designed and informative two-page info sheet from Gender Justice in Early Childhood provides an overview of gender, research about gender-expansive children, and information on the importance of gender-inclusive environments. Useful for family education initiatives.

CHILDREN'S BOOK LISTS

Gender-Inclusive Classrooms Book List

https://www.genderinclassrooms.com/books

GLSEN Book List

https://www.glsen.org/sites/default/files/2021-07/GLSEN_NSC_Booklist_ Elementary_2021.pdf

Institute for Anti-Racist Education LGBTQ+ Affirming Books for Kindergarten and First Grade Book List

https://bookshop.org/lists/lgbtq-affirming-books-for-kindergarten-1st-grade

Welcoming Schools Book Lists

https://www.welcomingschools.org/resources/books/

CURRICULUM RESOURCES AND LESSON PLANS

Darlene Tando's Gender Worksheet for Kids

https://darlenetandogenderblog.files.wordpress.com/2017/08/ newworksheet2019.pdf

This one-page worksheet was designed by Darlene Tando, LCSW, a San Diego–based gender therapist who works with children and families. She is the author of *The Conscious Parent's Guide to Gender Identity: A Mindful Approach to Embracing Your Child's Authentic Self* (2016). You can find Darlene's explanation of how to use this worksheet with children through this link:

https://darlenetandogenderblog.com/2017/08/03/new-and-improved-gender-worksheet-for-kids/

Gender-Inclusive Classrooms

https://www.genderinclassrooms.com/

Website for teachers providing gender-inclusive curriculum, book suggestions, and support. Curriculum and reading guides, including for the early years, are available in addition to other resources. Gender-Inclusive Classrooms also has an active Instagram account. Highly recommended resource for teachers.

Gender Justice in Early Childhood

https://www.genderjusticeinearlychildhood.com/

Organization working to support and educate about gender justice in early childhood through "community engaged scholarship, training, resource creation, and more." Provides resources and support based on the content of *Supporting Gender Diversity in Early Childhood Classrooms,* a book written by the Gender Justice in Early Childhood team.

The Gender Wheel

http://www.genderwheel.com/

This website offers curriculum and materials to support the lessons and concepts in Maya Gonzalez's books, including *The Gender Wheel.* Pronoun games, teacher tips, trainings, curriculum and lesson plans, and more are included on this website. A solid resource for teachers to explore.

The Safe Zone Project

https://thesafezoneproject.com/

The Safe Zone Project provides free curriculum resources for educators. The website provides tools to empower educators to train others and create safe zones and inclusivity in their programs.

Trans Student Educational Resources (TSER)

http://transstudent.org/

TSER focuses on creating a more welcoming and affirming educational system through resources, trainings, and curriculum. Youth-led, TSER produces resources such as the Gender Unicorn, as well as conducting leadership trainings and policy work.

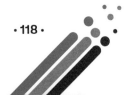

Welcoming Schools

http://www.welcomingschools.org/

An offshoot of the Human Rights Campaign, Welcoming Schools is one of the most abundant sources of relevant resources for teachers, administrators, and school programs looking for resources and support in improving their gender-affirming practices. This highly organized and well-designed website offers excellent resources including one-sheets, handouts, reading lists, lesson plans, tips, trainings, and more. Highly recommended.

GENERAL RESOURCES FOR EDUCATORS

Gay, Lesbian, and Straight Education Network (GLSEN)

http://www.glsen.org

National organization committed to supporting educators to support their students, as well as raise up youth-led initiatives and programs. GLSEN conducts research, provides curricular resources and other support to teachers, and acts as an advocacy organization for policy and legislative change. Website contains many resources for educators.

Gender Diversity

http://www.genderdiversity.org/

A nonprofit organization providing conferences, trainings, PD, and family support services for those who are, love, or work with gender-diverse people. Gender Diversity is the leading group behind the Gender Odyssey national conference each year.

Gender Spectrum

https://www.genderspectrum.org/

Advocacy organization working to provide supportive environments for gender-diverse children and teens. Website offers a wealth of information, including resources, professional development, and support for educators.

Human Rights Campaign

https://www.hrc.org/resources

The HRC website offers specific resources for transgender children and teens, including research, advocacy, reports, and more. A reputable and widely recognized organization with a wealth of resources for individuals and groups. Another page has specific links for making schools more gender inclusive: https://www.hrc.org/blog/five-must-have-resources-to-make-back-to-school-gender-inclusive

REFERENCE/RESOURCE BOOKS AND REPORTS

Angello, Michele, and Ali Bowman. 2016. *Raising the Transgender Child: A Complete Guide for Parents, Families, and Caregivers*. Berkeley, CA: Seal Press.

Practical guide aimed at parents that is clear, straightforward, and reassuring. Covers aspects of development and needs of the gender-diverse child, including personal and social-emotional needs; legal, education, and medical concerns; and resources.

Baum, Joel, et al. n.d. *Supporting and Caring for Our Gender Expansive Youth: Lessons from the Human Rights Campaign's Youth Survey*. Human Rights Campaign. https://assets2.hrc.org/files/assets/resources/Gender-expansive-youth-report-final.pdf

Extensive report summarizing the findings from a large-scale survey of gender-expansive youth, with subsequent recommendations for caregivers and parents.

Bianchi, Anna. 2017. *Becoming an Ally to the Gender-Expansive Child: A Guide for Parents and Carers*. Philadelphia, PA: Jessica Kingsley Publishers.

Written from the perspective of a grandmother with a trans granddaughter, the author empathetically presents the case for allyship. The author is British, so some UK–specific references and resources are included, but very applicable to all parents and teachers regardless of place of residence. Recommended for family and friends.

Brill, Stephanie, and Rachel Pepper. 2008. *The Transgender Child: A Handbook for Families and Professionals*. Minneapolis, MN: Cleis Press.

One of the foremost resources about transgender children. Primary audience is parents, but chapters and information are particularly relevant for educators and caregivers as well.

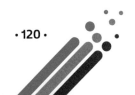

Bryan, Jennifer. 2012. *From the Dress-Up Corner to the Senior Prom: Navigating Gender and Sexuality Diversity in PreK–12 Schools*. Lanham, MD: Rowman and Littlefield Education.

Excellent resource for teachers interested in making their classrooms more accepting of gender diversity. Full of examples, questions, and reflective exercises, and written in a digestible manner, this book serves as a tool for teachers to reflect on their own practice and expand their planning and views.

Ehrensaft, Diane. 2016. *The Gender Creative Child: Pathways for Nurturing and Supporting Children Who Live Outside Gender Boxes*. New York: The Experiment.

Written to guide parents and professionals in supporting gender-expansive children with a focus on exploring how gender can be fluid.

Erickson-Schroth, Laura, and Laura A. Jacobs. 2017. *"You're in the Wrong Bathroom!" and 20 Other Myths and Misconceptions about Transgender and Gender-Nonconforming People*. Boston, MA: Beacon Press.

Informational and accessible *book* including reality-based research as well as basic knowledge and terminology presented in a nonjudgmental way. Recommended as a good start to help readers confront their own biases and misconceptions, while creating a more respectful and realistic understanding of gender.

Gonzales, Kathryn, and Karen Rayne. 2019. *Trans+: Love, Sex, Romance, and Being You*. Washington, DC: Magination Press.

Guidebook published by the American Psychological Association and written for teens in a conversational, matter-of-fact, informative style. Although the target audience is teens who are gender diverse, this is an approachable and informative resource for parents, teachers, and others looking to understand gender in a frank and sympathetic way.

Harris, Robie. 2006. *It's Not The Stork! A Book about Boys, Girls, Babies, Bodies, Families, and Friends*. Somerville, MA: Candlewick Press.

Aimed at ages four and up, this age-appropriate explanation of bodies and reproduction is an essential resource for parents or teachers who need assistance explaining anatomy, physiology, or reproduction in a developmentally appropriate, body-positive way. Companion books are *It's So Amazing* (for elementary schoolers) and *It's Perfectly Normal* (for preteens and teens). A highly recommended series.

Human Rights Campaign Foundation and Welcoming Schools. 2019. *Be Prepared for LGBTQ Questions and Concerns.* Human Rights Campaign Foundation and Welcoming Schools.

This three-page handout offers guidance, research, and strategies for responding to parents and coworkers. https://assets2.hrc.org/welcoming-schools/documents/WS_Responding_to_Concerns.pdf

National Center on Parent, Family, and Community Engagement. n.d. *Healthy Gender Development and Young Children: A Guide for Early Childhood Programs and Professionals*. Washington, DC: U.S Department of Health and Human Services, Administration for Children and Families. https://eclkc.ohs.acf.hhs.gov/sites/default/files/pdf/healthy-gender-development.pdf

This report prepared for the National Head Start Association outlines typical gender development, showing sensitivity for behaviors and play that defy gender stereotypes. While the focus is not specifically on gender-diverse children, the report offers specific scenarios and suggestions for ECE professionals on how to respond to common concerns and questions, as well as resources.

Orr, Asaf, et al. n.d. *Schools in Transition: A Guide for Supporting Transgender Students in K–12 Schools*. New York: ACLU. https://www.aclu.org/sites/default/files/field_document/schools_in_transition_6.3.16.pdf

This sixty-eight-page guide produced by the ACLU, Gender Spectrum, the Human Rights Campaign, NEA, and NCLR provides guidance for school staff to assist them in supporting students. While it is focused on K–12 programs, many of the general concepts and policy suggestions are relevant for ECE programs as well.

Pastel, Encian, et al. 2019. *Supporting Gender Diversity in Early Childhood Classrooms: A Practical Guide*. Philadelphia, PA: Jessica Kingsley Publishers.

Practical guide written by the team behind *Gender Justice in Early Childhood*, this new book offers practical steps for caregivers and early childhood educators. Focus on self-reflection and auditing to build supportive skills. Strong resource for ECE teachers and programs.

Storck, Kelly, and Noah Grigni. 2018. *The Gender-Identity Workbook for Kids: A Guide to Exploring Who You Are*. Oakland, CA: Instant Help Books.

Aimed at five- to twelve-year-olds, this workbook/guide with dozens of simple activities is designed to help children explore their understanding of gender and identity. The book is designed for those who are gender creative, but many of the ideas and activities would be easily adapted for general use in an ECE classroom to use with children who are cisgender or for adults to help explore their own understanding. Provides ideas for teachers and parents to open discussion around gender and can also be used independently by older children.

APPENDIX B: RECOMMENDED CHILDREN'S BOOKS

Anderson, Airlie. 2018. *Neither*. Boston, MA: Little, Brown Books for Young Readers.

In a land of blue bunnies and yellow birds, a green hybrid creature hatches and challenges everyone's ideas of what makes them similar and different.

Arnold, Elana K. 2019. *What Riley Wore*. San Diego, CA: Beach Lane Books.

Riley wears all kinds of different clothes and costumes, depending on the day and how Riley is feeling. Focus of the story is on the positives of how each outfit makes Riley feel and how others positively react to Riley's clothes. Good for the ECE classroom library.

Davids, Stacy B. 2015. *Annie's Plaid Shirt*. North Miami Beach, FL: Upswing Press.

Annie does not want to wear a dress to her uncle's wedding and comes up with a clever solution to make sure she can be herself. Good exploration of themes related to gender exploration and expression, respect, and individuality.

Feder, Tyler. 2021. *Bodies Are Cool*. New York: Dial Books for Young Readers.

Colorful, busy scenes illustrate rhyming, body-positive prose, allowing readers the opportunity to energetically engage in an inclusive celebration of all types of bodies.

Ford, JR, and Vanessa Ford. 2021. *Calvin*. New York: G.P. Putnam's Sons Books for Young Readers.

In this happy story, Calvin is supported by family, school, and friends when she lets them know she is a boy. A gentle and heartwarming portrayal of a child coming out as transgender.

Gehl, Laura. 2019. *Except When They Don't*. New York: Little Bee Books.

Rhyming prose and bright illustrations upend gender norms and remind children to be exactly who they are.

Genhart, Michael. 2019. *Rainbow: A First Book of Pride*. Washington, DC: Magination Press.

Simple picture book exploring the colors of the rainbow flag by depicting diverse children, adults, and family structures.

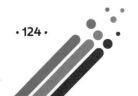

Gonzalez, Maya Christina, and Matthew SG. 2019. *They She He Me: Easy as ABC*. Reflection Press.

Uses an ABC book format to introduce diverse children (and their pronouns!) with a variety of interests.

Gonzalez, Maya Christina, and Matthew SG. 2017. *They She He Me: Free to Be!* San Francisco, CA: Reflection Press.

A great tool to start and continue pronoun conversations with young children. Depicting multiple gender expressions and identities under many different pronouns, this simple book is a valuable conversation starter and guide while maintaining the focus on the value of personal expression.

Hall, Michael. 2015. *Red: A Crayon's Story*. New York: Greenwillow Books.

The story of a blue crayon with a red wrapper who can't live up to the expectation that he is red. When he is finally allowed to be blue, it is better for everyone! Age-appropriate and realistic way to explore feelings related to not fitting in. Recommended for the ECE classroom library.

Hoffman, Mary. 2011. *The Great Big Book of Families*. New York: Dial Books for Young Readers.

Richly illustrated treasury exploring aspects of family life, with each spread encompassing a huge variety of family diversity. A great addition to a classroom library to encourage belonging and identification and spur conversation.

John, Jory. The Critter Jitters series. New York: Dial Books for Young Readers

A nice series of books with no use of gender pronouns or gender markers for the characters.

Bright illustrations show how a class of diverse animals navigates new experiences such as the first day of school and sleepaway camp. The characters find ways to cope that are perfect for their individual needs.

Johnson, Chelsea, LaToya Council, and Carolyn Choi. 2021. *Intersection Allies: We Make Room for All*. New York: Dottir Press.

Papercut illustrations and clear prose show a close-knit, diverse neighborhood community moving through their days supporting and helping one another. A great introduction to what it means to be socially conscious and to the power of finding ways to help and connect with others in your own community. Includes a page-by-page discussion guide for adults.

Locke, Katherine. 2021. *What Are Your Words? A Book about Pronouns*. Boston, MA: Little Brown and Company.

A colorful introduction to gender pronouns through the experience of Ari, who is figuring out which words work best for them.

Love, Jessica. 2018. *Julián Is a Mermaid*. Somerville, MA: Candlewick Press.

Beautifully illustrated story of Julián, who makes his own mermaid costume after seeing three beautiful mermaids (people in drag) on the subway. His abuela (grandmother) takes him to join the other mermaids in a parade. Good opportunity to discuss pride and self-expression.

Lukoff, Kyle. 2019. *Call Me Max*. New York: Reycraft Books.

Max is a transgender boy who shares about his life at school, home, and with friends. Provides a clear, easy-to-understand explanation of being transgender, with some coverage of concerns and issues relevant to early elementary. The first in a series. Perfect for a classroom with trans students.

Madison, Megan, and Jessica Ralli. 2021. *Being You: A First Conversation about Gender*. New York: Penguin.

Colorful illustrations and simple text lead to open-ended questions meant to trigger discussion related to personal identity, pronouns, and gender. The board book is appropriate for ages three to seven and includes supporting information for adults to help them in the conversation.

Moradian, Afsaneh. 2018. *Jamie Is Jamie: A Book about Being Yourself and Playing Your Way*. Minneapolis, MN: Free Spirit Publishing.

Jamie engages in all types of play with both boys and girls at school. Classmates wonder, "Is Jamie a girl or a boy?" and ultimately decide that it doesn't matter. Jamie is a fun friend. Tips for teachers and parents about encouraging and supporting free, nongendered play are included at the end of the story.

O'Leary, Sara. 2016. *A Family Is a Family Is a Family*. Toronto, ON: Groundwood Books. O'Leary, Sara. 2021. *A Kid Is a Kid Is a Kid*. Toronto, ON: Groundwood Books.

In *A Family Is a Family Is a Family*, a classroom full of children explores the ways their families are different, similar, and special. *A Kid Is a Kid Is a Kid* examines intrusive or gendered questions faced by children, with a focus on what children really want to be asked, such as, "Do you want to play?"

Patterson, Jodie. 2021. *Born Ready: The True Story of a Boy Named Penelope*. New York: Crown Books for Young Readers.

An exploration of one child's transition to making sure that others see and understand him for who he is. A good fit for classrooms with trans students.

Penfold, Alexandra. 2018. *All Are Welcome*. New York: Knopf Books for Young Readers.

This simple rhyming story depicts a classroom/school where inclusion and diversity are valued. Colorful images show children and families of different backgrounds, abilities, races, and more. A good book for opening conversations about inclusion of all types.

Pessin-Whedbee, Brook. 2017. *Who Are You? The Kid's Guide to Gender Identity*. Philadelphia, PA: Jessica Kingsley Publishers.

Written to the reader in the second person, this book is designed to explain gender identity and help children understand the fluidity of difference by understanding their own gender expression and identity. Simple, straightforward, affirming text with colorful illustrations. Includes a guide for adults including discussion points for preschool and elementary age children, resources, and an interactive gender wheel that allows readers to explore their own body, identity, and expression. Recommended for families or classrooms where gender identity is an area of discussion.

Spanyol, Jessica. (various dates). All about Rosa series and All about Clive series. London, UK: Child's Play International, Ltd.

These board books challenge gender stereotypes and celebrate various interests, inclusivity, and gender equality. Titles in the series include *Rosa Loves Cars, Rosa Plays Ball, Rosa Loves Dinosaurs, Clive and His Babies, Clive and His Bags, Clive and His Art*. Perfect for a toddler classroom due to the simple stories and board-book format.

APPENDIX C:
RESOURCES FOR PARENTS AND FAMILIES

WEBSITES
Gender Diversity

http://www.genderdiversity.org/

A nonprofit organization providing conferences, trainings, professional development, and family-support services for those who are, love, or work with gender-diverse people. Gender Diversity is the leading group behind the Gender Odyssey national conference each year.

Gender Spectrum

https://www.genderspectrum.org/

An advocacy organization working to provide supportive environments for gender-diverse children and teens. The website offers a wealth of information, including resources, professional development, and support for educators.

GLAAD

https://www.glaad.org/transgender

GLAAD is one of the most visible and largest LGBTQ+ advocacy organizations, working to advance cultural change related to LGBTQ+ issues. Their website includes a host of resources, including many specific to transgender issues.

Human Rights Campaign

https://www.hrc.org/resources

The HRC website offers specific resources for transgender children and teens, including research, advocacy, reports, and more. A reputable and widely recognized organization with a wealth of resources for individuals and groups. Another page has specific links for making schools more gender inclusive: https://www.hrc.org/blog/five-must-have-resources-to-make-back-to-school-gender-inclusive

interACT Advocates for Intersex Youth

https://interactadvocates.org_

This organization supports children born with intersex traits. InterACT works to develop medical and legal policies, collaborate on research, and advocate for the human rights of children with variations of sex development.

PFLAG

https://www.pflag.org

A nationwide family support group, PFLAG has grown to incorporate community action as well. Website includes numerous resources for parents, family, and friends of children who are LGBTQ.

TransFamilies

https://transfamilies.org/

An offshoot of Gender Spectrum, TransFamilies offers support and information to families with children who are trans or gender diverse. Run by families with personal experience with gender diversity, the TransFamilies website provides a supportive collection of resources and services for families.

TransFamily Support Services

https://www.transfamilysos.org/

A San Diego County, California, organization that provides support groups, legal and insurance assistance, speaking engagements, and school/workplace trainings related to supporting and affirming children who are gender diverse. A local resource that provides a wealth of knowledge and connection.

In addition to the organizations listed, many local and regional organizations work to support LGBTQIA+ individuals and families through support groups, resource shares, education, and more. Depending on where you live, you may find some great local resources that would be great additions to your parent-resource lists and library.

BOOKS

Ehrensaft, Diane. 2011. *Gender Born, Gender Made: Raising Healthy Gender-Nonconforming Children*. New York: The Experiment.

This book aimed at families provides methods for supporting gender-diverse children from a psychologically supported viewpoint. Presents an affirming and supportive model focused on gender creativity and fluidity.

Tando, Darlene. 2016. *The Conscious Parent's Guide to Gender Identity: A Mindful Approach to Embracing Your Child's Authentic Self*. New York: Adams Media.

A well-known therapist who specializes in children who are trans and gender creative authored this book aimed at helping parents navigate their parenting journey with a gender-creative child. Extensive and full of resources and specific tips and strategies.

REFERENCES

Allvin, Rhian E. 2018. "Embracing Equity: Helping All Children Reach Their Full Potential." *Young Children* 73(2): 4–9.

American Psychological Association. n.d. *How Educators Can Support Families with Gender Diverse and Sexual Minority Youth: Promoting Resiliency for Gender Diverse and Sexual Minority Students in Schools.* Washington, DC: APA. https://www.apa.org/pi/lgbt/programs/safe-supportive/lgbt/educators-families.pdf

American Psychological Association and National Association of School Psychologists. 2015. *Resolution on Gender and Sexual Orientation Diversity in Children and Adolescents in Schools.* Washington, DC: American Psychological Association. https://www.apa.org/about/policy/orientation-diversity

Angello, Michele, and Ali Bowman. 2016. *Raising the Transgender Child: A Complete Guide for Parents, Families, and Caregivers.* Berkeley, CA: Seal Press.

Baum, Joel, et al. n.d. *Supporting and Caring for Our Gender Expansive Youth: Lessons from the Human Rights Campaign's Youth Survey.* Human Rights Campaign. https://assets2.hrc.org/files/assets/resources/Gender-expansive-youth-report-final.pdf?_ga=2.131109963.579601291.1647876084-791608059.1647876084

Bianchi, Anna. 2017. *Becoming an Ally to the Gender-Expansive Child: A Guide for Parents and Carers.* Philadelphia, PA: Jessica Kingsley Publishers.

Blackless, Melanie, et al. 2000. "How Sexually Dimorphic Are We? Review and Synthesis." *American Journal of Human Biology* 12(2): 151–166.

Brill, Stephanie, and Rachel Pepper. 2008. *The Transgender Child: A Handbook for Families and Professionals*. Minneapolis, MN: Cleis Press.

Bussey, Kay, and Albert Bandura. 1999. "Social Cognitive Theory of Gender Development and Differentiation." *Psychological Review* 106(4): 676–713.

California Department of Education. 2019. Health Education Framework. California Department of Education. https://www.cde.ca.gov/ci/he/cf/

Carter, Michael J. 2014. "Gender Socialization and Identity Theory." *Social Sciences* 3(2): 242–263.

Cory, Abbie, Jenny Fererro, and Hossna Sadat Ahadi. 2021. "She, They, He, Us: Transforming Campus Inclusivity Through the Use of Pronouns." Academic Senate for California Community Colleges. https://www.asccc.org/content/she-they-he-us-transforming-campus-inclusivity-through-use-pronouns

Derman-Sparks, Louise, and the ABC Task Force. 1989. *Anti-Bias Curriculum: Tools for Empowering Young Children*. Washington, DC: NAEYC.

Derman-Sparks, Louise, Debbie LeeKeenan, and John Nimmo. 2015. *Leading Anti-Bias Early Childhood Programs: A Guide for Change.* New York: Teachers College Press and Washington, DC: NAEYC.

Derman-Sparks, Louise, and Julie Olsen Edwards. 2010. *Anti-Bias Education for Young Children and Ourselves.* Washington, DC: NAEYC.

Derman-Sparks, Louise, Julie Olsen Edwards, and Catherine Goins. 2020. *Anti-Bias Education for Young Children and Ourselves.* 2nd edition. Washington, DC: NAEYC.

Dombro, Amy Laura, Judy Jablon, and Charlotte Stetson. 2011. *Powerful Interactions: How to Connect with Children to Extend Their Learning.* Washington, DC: NAEYC.

Ehrensaft, Diane. 2016. *The Gender Creative Child: Pathways for Nurturing and Supporting Children Who Live Outside Gender Boxes*. New York: The Experiment.

Ellis Nutt, Amy. 2016. *Becoming Nicole: The Transformation of an American Family*. New York: Random House.

GUIDANCE FOR SUPPORTING **GENDER DIVERSITY** IN EARLY CHILDHOOD EDUCATION

Gülgöz, Selin, et al. 2019. "Similarity in Transgender and Cisgender Children's Gender Development." *PNAS* 116(49): 24480–24485.

Halim, May Ling D., Danielle Bryant, and Kenneth J. Zucker. 2016. "Early Gender Development in Children and Links with Mental and Physical Health." In *Health Promotion for Children and Adolescents*. New York: Springer.

Herman, Jody L., et al. 2017. "Age of Individuals Who Identify as Transgender in the United States." UCLA School of Law Williams Institute. https://williamsinstitute.law.ucla.edu/publications/age-trans-individuals-us/

Human Rights Campaign Foundation and Welcoming Schools. 2019. *Be Prepared for LGBTQ Questions and Concerns*. Human Rights Campaign and Welcoming Schools. https://assets2.hrc.org/welcoming-schools/documents/WS_Responding_to_Concerns.pdf

James, Sandy E., et al. 2016. *The Report of the 2015 U.S. Transgender Survey*. Washington, DC: National Center for Transgender Equality. https://transequality.org/sites/default/files/docs/usts/USTS-Full-Report-Dec17.pdf

Joel, Daphna, and Luba Vikhanski. 2019. *Gender Mosaic: Beyond the Myth of the Male and Female Brain*. New York: Little, Brown Spark.

Johns, Michelle M., et al. 2019. *Transgender Identity and Experiences of Violence Victimization, Substance Use, Suicide Risk, and Sexual Risk Behaviors Among High School Students—19 States and Large Urban School Districts, 2017*. Centers for Disease Control and Prevention. Morbidity and Mortality Weekly Report. 2019(68): 67–71. https://www.cdc.gov/mmwr/volumes/68/wr/mm6803a3.htm

Kroeger, Janice, Abigail Recker, and Alexandra Gunn. 2019. "Tate and the Pink Coat: Exploring Gender and Enacting Anti-Bias Principles." *Young Children* 74(1): 83–92.

LGBTQ+ Resource Center. 2022. "Why Is It Important to Respect People's Pronouns?" University of Wisconsin, Milwaukee. https://uwm.edu/lgbtrc/qa_faqs/why-is-it-important-to-respect-peoples-pronouns/

Mangione, Peter L. 2017. "The PITC Past, Present, and Future: Reflecting on the Meaning of Respectful, Responsive Relationships in the Care of Infants and Toddlers." Presented March 2 at SCPITC Advanced Training, Isle of

Palms, SC. https://scpitc.org/wp-content/uploads/2017/03/Mangione-Presentation_3-2-17.pdf

Martin, Carol L., and Diane N. Ruble. 2010. "Patterns of Gender Development." *Annual Review of Psychology* 61: 353–381.

Martin, Carol L., Diane N. Ruble, and Joel Szkrybalo. 2002. "Cognitive Theories of Early Gender Development." *Psychological Bulletin* 128(6): 903–933.

McCulloch, Jeffrey. 2019. "Supporting Gender Expansive Children and Families in the Preschool Classroom." *Exchange* 41(2).

Miller, Cynthia L., Barbara A. Younger, and Philip A. Morse. 1982. "The Categorization of Male and Female Voices in Infancy." *Infant Behavior and Development* 5(2–4): 143–159.

Murchison, Gabe, et al. 2016. *Supporting and Caring for Transgender Children*. Washington, DC: Human Rights Campaign Foundation. https://assets2.hrc.org/files/documents/SupportingCaringforTransChildren.pdf

National Association for the Education of Young Children. 2011. *Code of Ethical Conduct and Statement of Commitment*. Position statement. Washington, DC: NAEYC. https://www.naeyc.org/sites/default/files/globally-shared/downloads/PDFs/resources/position-statements/Ethics%20Position%20Statement2011_09202013update.pdf

National Association for the Education of Young Children. 2019. *Advancing Equity in Early Childhood Education*. Position statement. Washington, DC: NAEYC. https://www.naeyc.org/sites/default/files/globally-shared/downloads/PDFs/resources/position-statements/advancingequitypositionstatement.pdf

National Association for the Education of Young Children. 2019. *Professional Standards and Competencies for Early Childhood Educators*. Position statement. Washington, DC: NAEYC. https://www.naeyc.org/sites/default/files/globally-shared/downloads/PDFs/resources/position-statements/standards_and_competencies_ps.pdf

National Association for the Education of Young Children. 2020. *Developmentally Appropriate Practice in Early Childhood Programs Serving Children from Birth through Age 8*. Position statement. Washington,

DC: NAEYC. https://www.naeyc.org/sites/default/files/globally-shared/downloads/PDFs/resources/position-statements/dap-statement_0.pdf

National Association of School Psychologists. 2014. *Safe Schools for Transgender and Gender Diverse Students.* Position statement. Bethesda, MD: NASP.

National Center on Parent, Family, and Community Engagement. n.d. *Healthy Gender Development And Young Children: A Guide For Early Childhood Programs And Professionals.* Washington, DC: US Department of Health and Human Services, Administration for Children and Families. https://eclkc.ohs.acf.hhs.gov/sites/default/files/pdf/healthy-gender-development.pdf

Nealy, Elijah C. 2019. *Trans Kids and Teens: Pride, Joy, and Families in Transition.* New York: W. W. Norton and Company.

Oregon Department of Education. n.d. *Sexuality Education: Frequently Asked Questions.* Oregon.gov. https://www.oregon.gov/ode/students-and-family/healthsafety/documents/sexedfaq.pdf

Orenstein, Gabriel A., and Lindsay Lewis. 2021. "Erikson's Stages of Psychosocial Development." Bethesda, MD: National Center for Biotechnology Information. https://www.ncbi.nlm.nih.gov/books/NBK556096/

Orr, Asaf, et al. n.d. *Schools in Transition: A Guide for Supporting Transgender Students in K–12 Schools.* New York: ACLU. https://www.aclu.org/sites/default/files/field_document/schools_in_transition_6.3.16.pdf

Pastel, Encian, et al. 2019. *Supporting Gender Diversity in Early Childhood Classrooms: A Practical Guide.* Philadelphia, PA: Jessica Kingsley Publishers.

Pessin-Whedbee, Brook. 2019. "Understanding Gender Diversity in Early Childhood." *Exchange* 41(2).

Peto, Andrea. 2011. "Supporting Transgender Children in the Primary Classroom: A Reflection." Gender and Education Association. http://www.genderandeducation.com/issues/supporting-transgender-children-in-the-primary-classroom/

Pickron, Charisse B., and Erik W. Cheries. 2019. "Infants' Individuation of Faces by Gender." *Brain Sciences* 9(7): 163.

Quinn, Paul C., et al. 2002. "Representation of the Gender of Human Faces by Infants: A Preference for Female." *Perception* 31(9): 1109–1121.

Rafferty, Jason, et al. 2018. "Ensuring Comprehensive Care and Support for Transgender and Gender-Diverse Children and Adolescents." *Pediatrics* 142(4): e20182162.

Roberts, Andrea L., et al. 2012. "Childhood Gender Nonconformity: A Risk Factor for Childhood Abuse and Posttraumatic Stress in Youth." *Pediatrics* 129(3): 410–417.

Ruble, Diane N., et al. 2007. "The Role of Gender Constancy in Early Gender Development." *Child Development* 78(4): 1121–1126.

SEICUS et al.. 2021. *A Call to Action: LGBTQ+ Youth Need Inclusive Sex Education*. URGE. https://urge.org/lgbtq-inclusive_sexed_report/

Spears Brown, Christia. 2014. *Parenting beyond Pink and Blue: How to Raise Your Kids Free of Gender Stereotypes*. Berkeley, CA: Ten Speed Press.

Steensma, Thomas D., et al. 2011. "Desisting and Persisting Gender Dysphoria after Childhood: A Qualitative Follow-Up Study." *Clinical Child Psychology and Psychiatry* 16(4): 499–516.

Steinmetz, Katy. 2016. "Why LGBT Advocates Say Bathroom 'Predators' Argument Is a Red Herring." May 2. *Time*. https://time.com/4314896/transgender-bathroom-bill-male-predators-argument/

Tordoff, Diana M., et al. 2022. "Mental Health Outcomes in Transgender and Nonbinary Youths Receiving Gender-Affirming Care." *JAMA Network Open* 5(2): e220978. https://jamanetwork.com/journals/jamanetworkopen/fullarticle/2789423

The Trevor Project. 2019. *The Trevor Project Research Brief: Data on Transgender Youth*. https://www.thetrevorproject.org/wp-content/uploads/2019/02/The-Trevor-Project-Research-Brief-February-2019.pdf

Virtual Lab School. n.d. *Creating Gender Safe Spaces*. Online training course. https://www.virtuallabschool.org/focused-topics/gender-safe

West, Alyssa. 2015. "A Brief Review of Cognitive Theories in Gender Development." *Behavioural Sciences Undergraduate Journal* 2(1): 59–66.

Yong, Ed. 2019. "Young Trans Children Know Who They Are." *The Atlantic*. https://www.theatlantic.com/science/archive/2019/01/young-trans-children-know-who-they-are/580366/

Zelazo, Philip D., Clancy B. Blair, and Michael T. Willoughby. 2017. *Executive Function: Implications for Education*. Washington, DC: U.S. Department of Education, Institute of Education Sciences. https://ies.ed.gov/ncer/pubs/20172000/pdf/20172000.pdf

Zosuls, Kristina M., et al. 2009. "The Acquisition of Gender Labels in Infancy: Implications for Gender-Typed Play." *Developmental Psychology* 45(3): 688–701.

INDEX

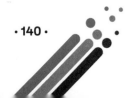

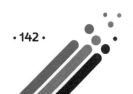

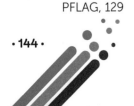